StoryBook Darlings

By Kelly Horton

For any further details, including information on other books or colouring pages contact:

Kellyartistthorton@yahoo.com

For more colouring pages:

www.etsy.com/uk/Colourcollectiveshop

Join the Facebook Community at

The Colouring Collective

StoryBook Darlings

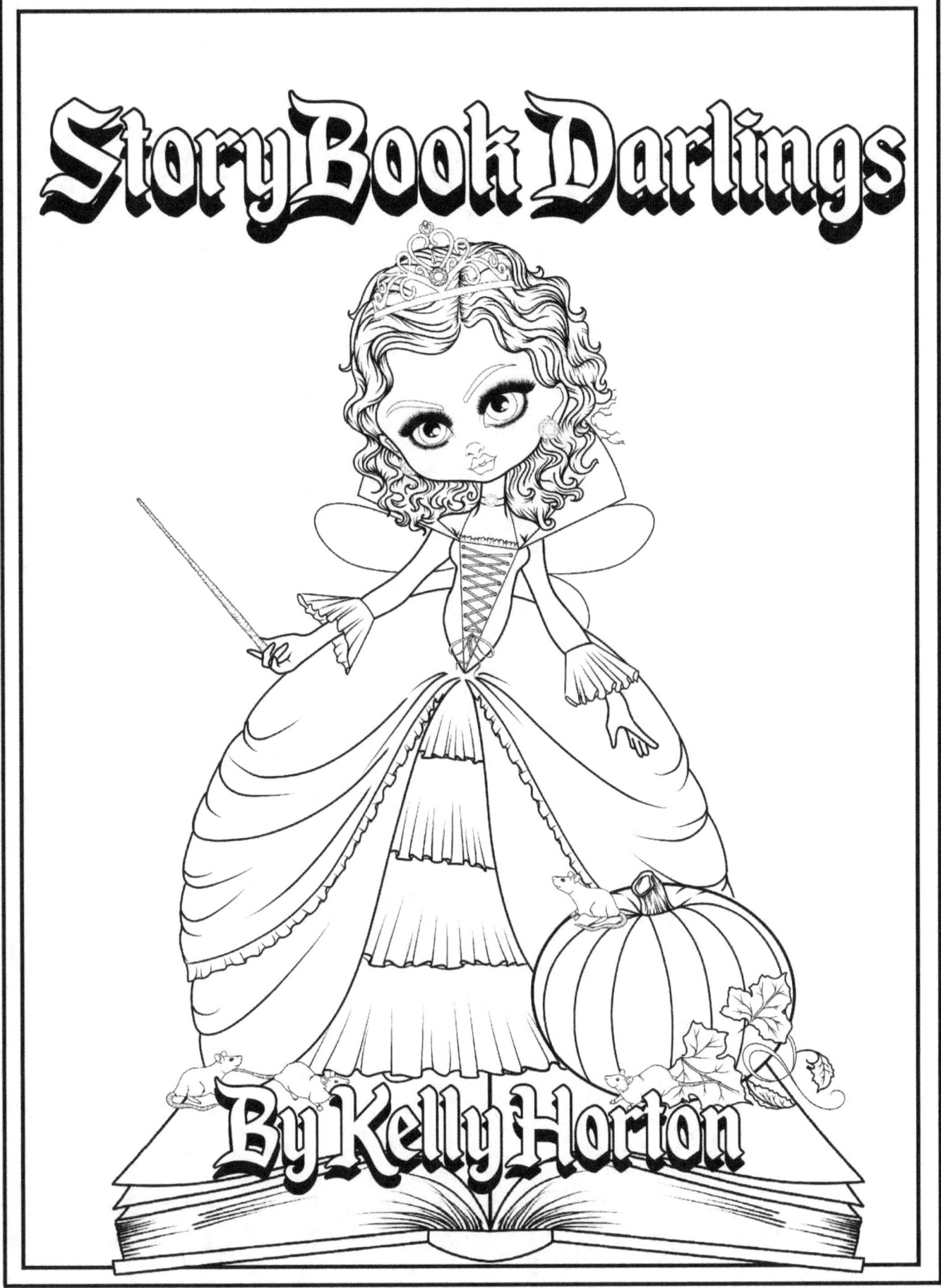

By Kelly Horton

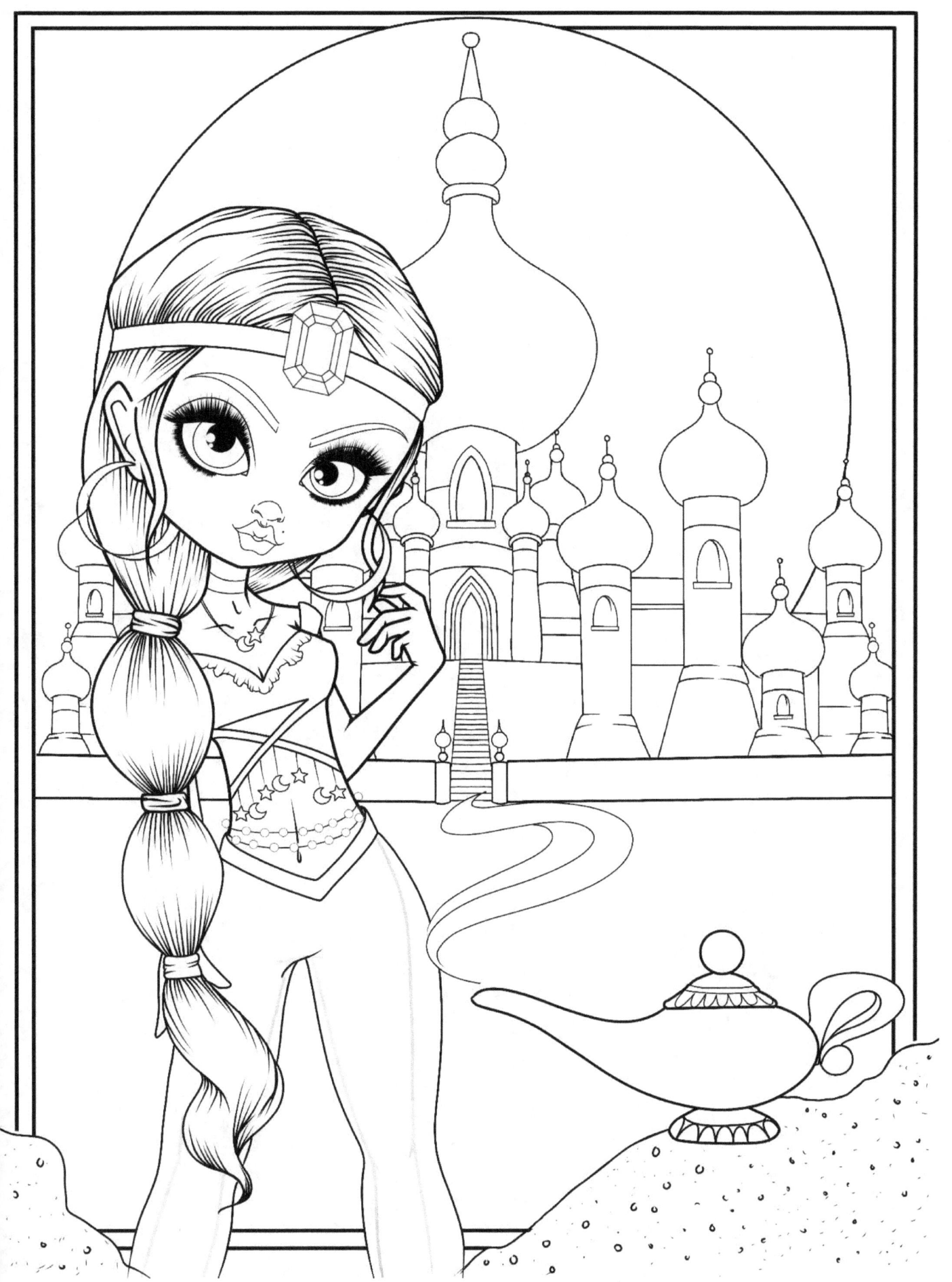

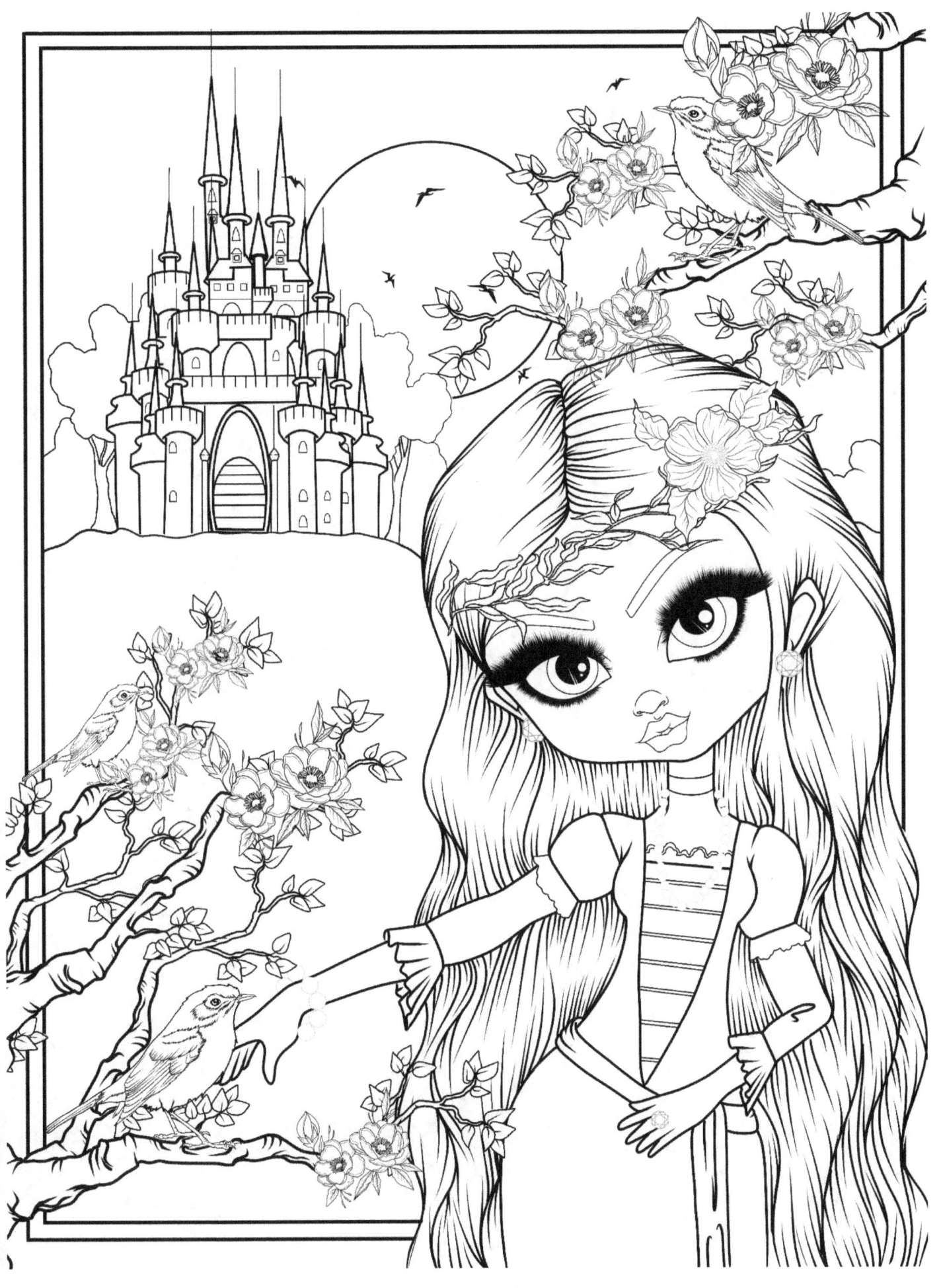

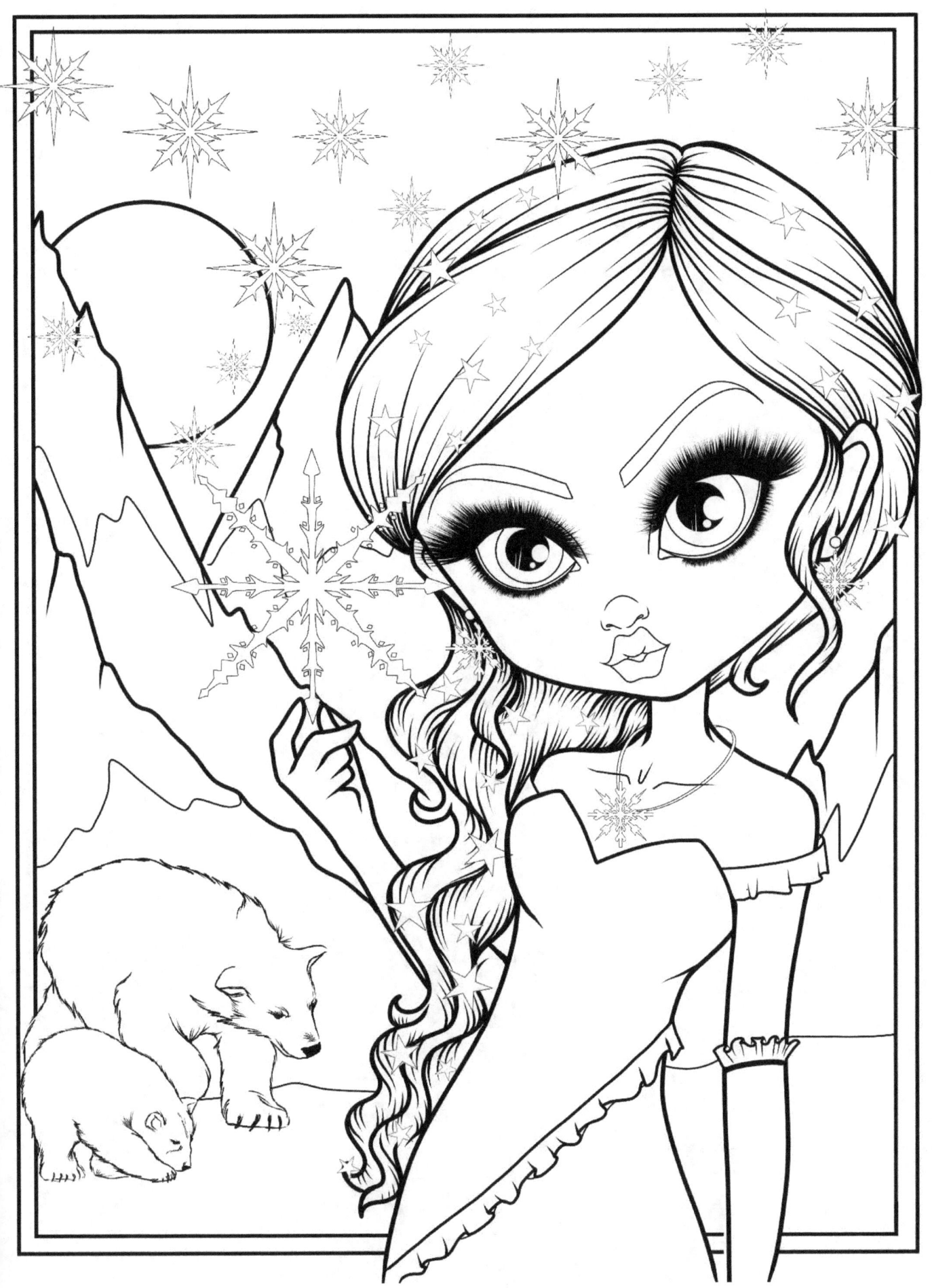

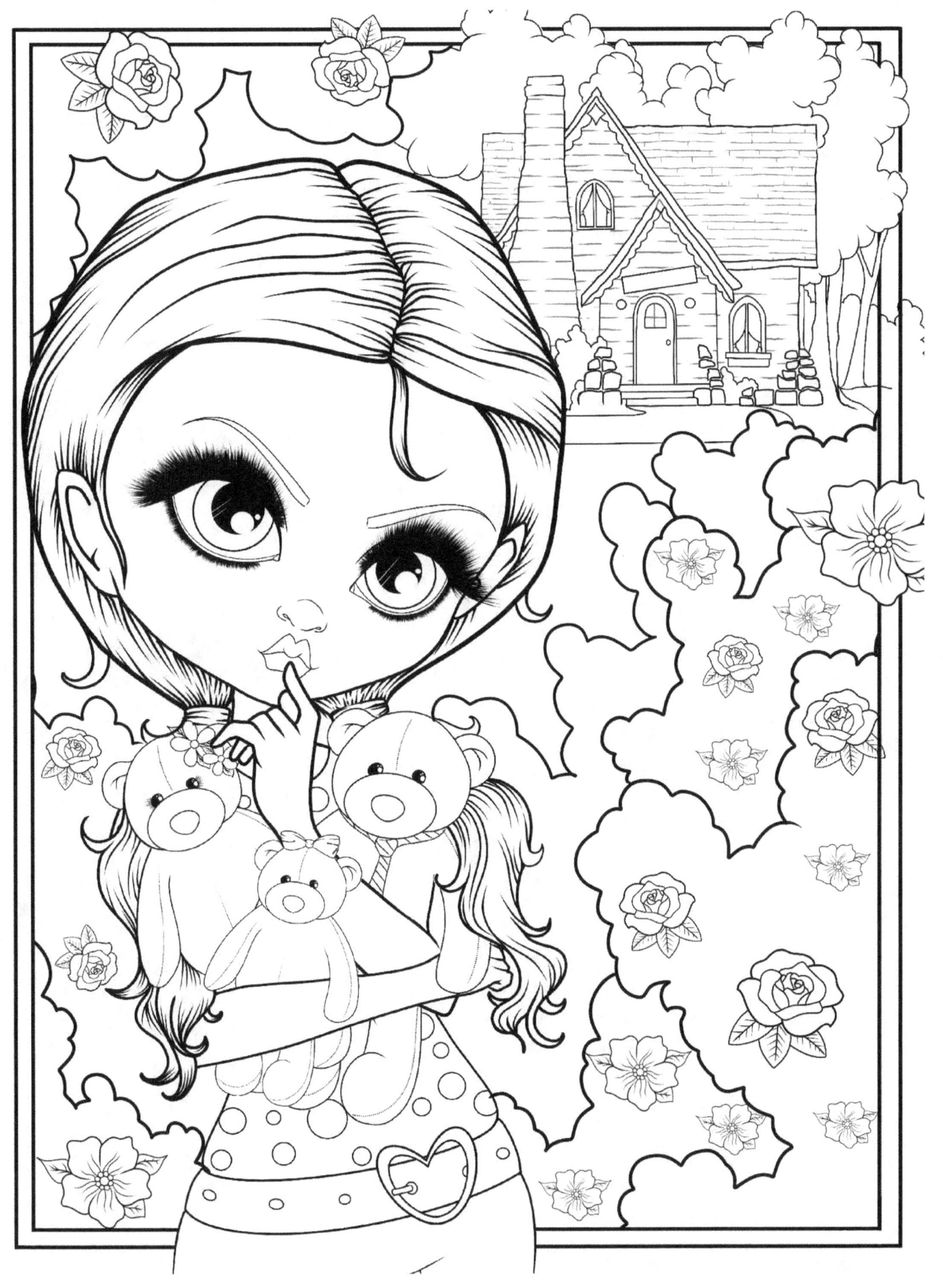

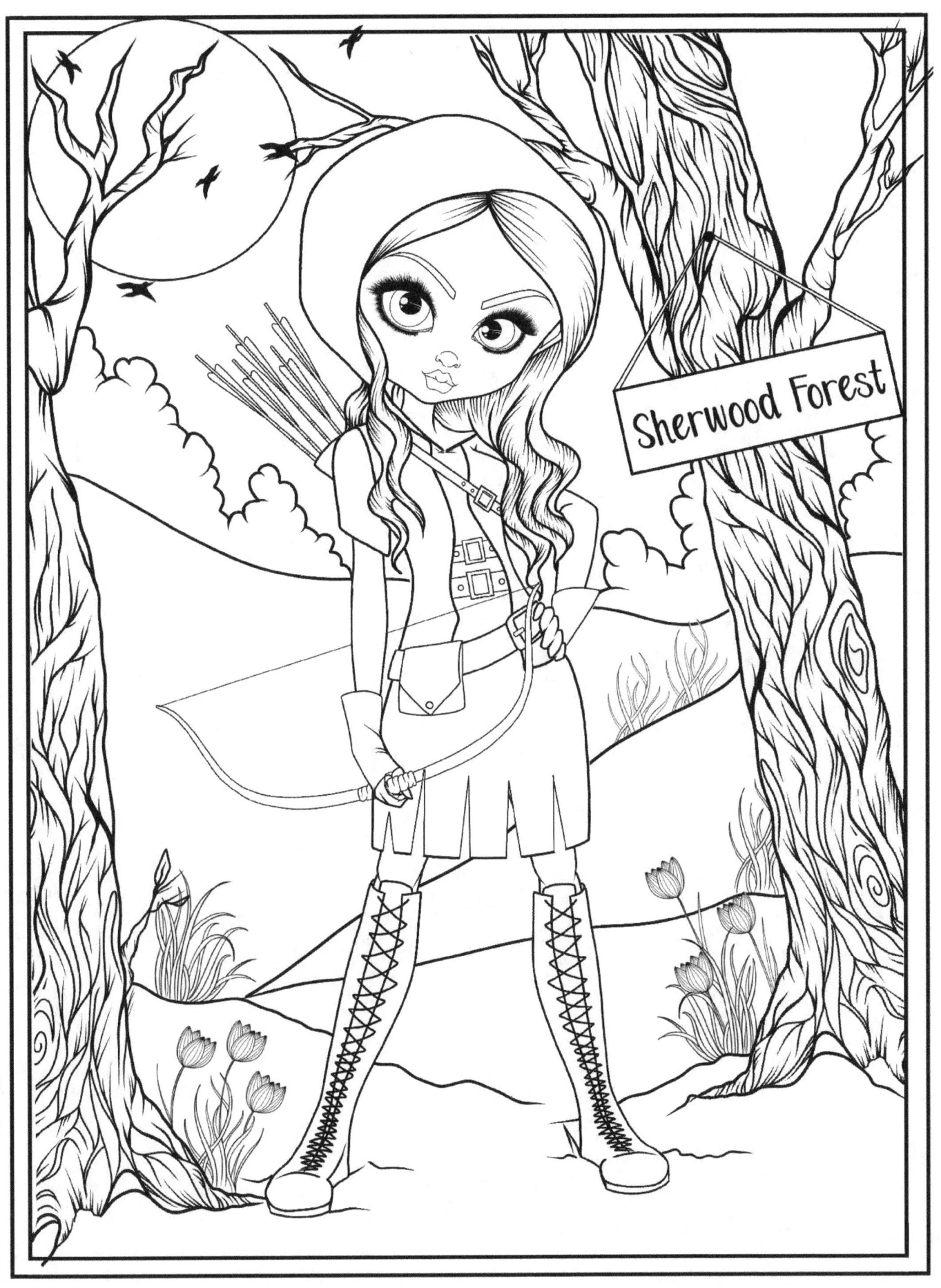

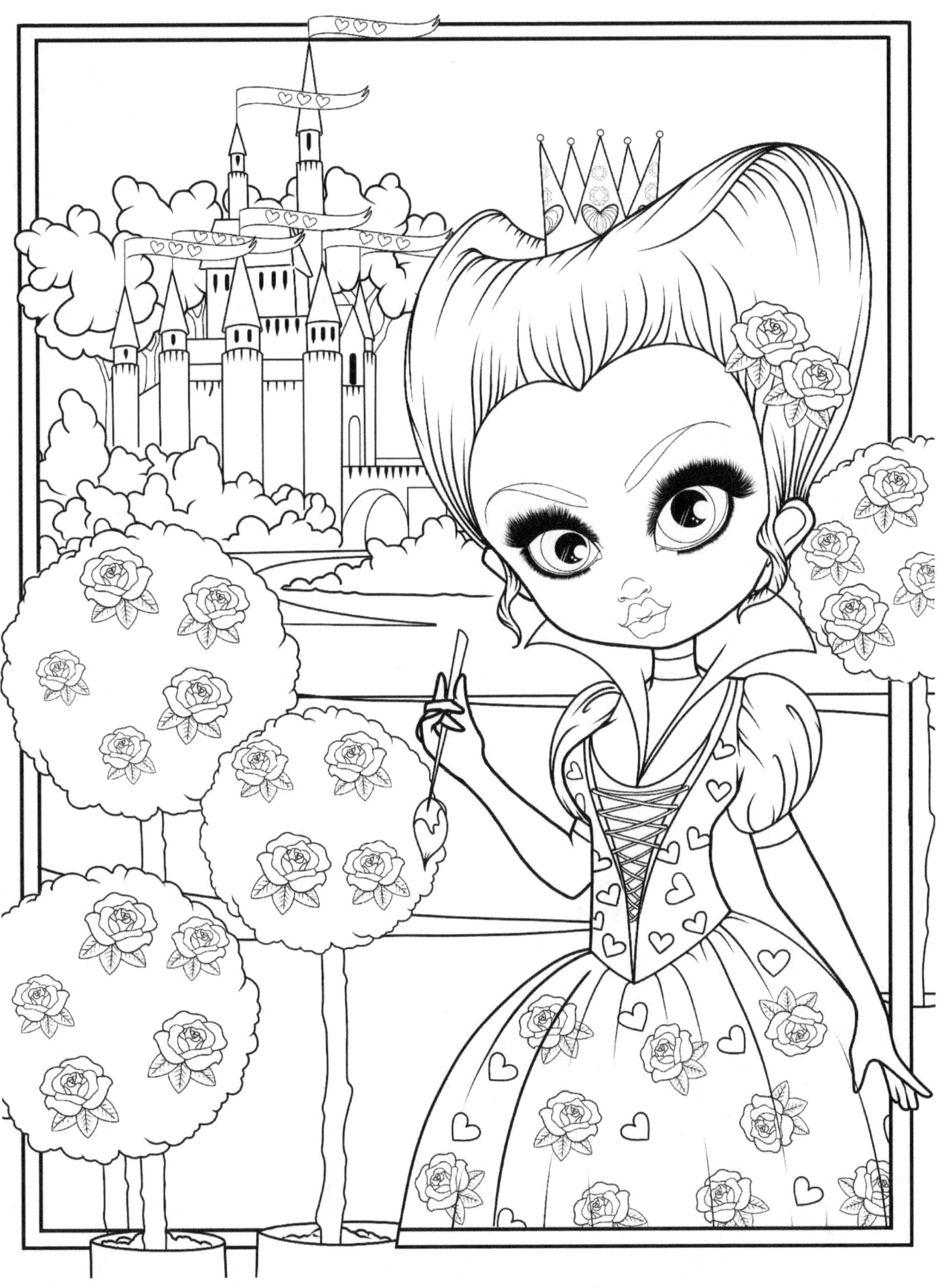

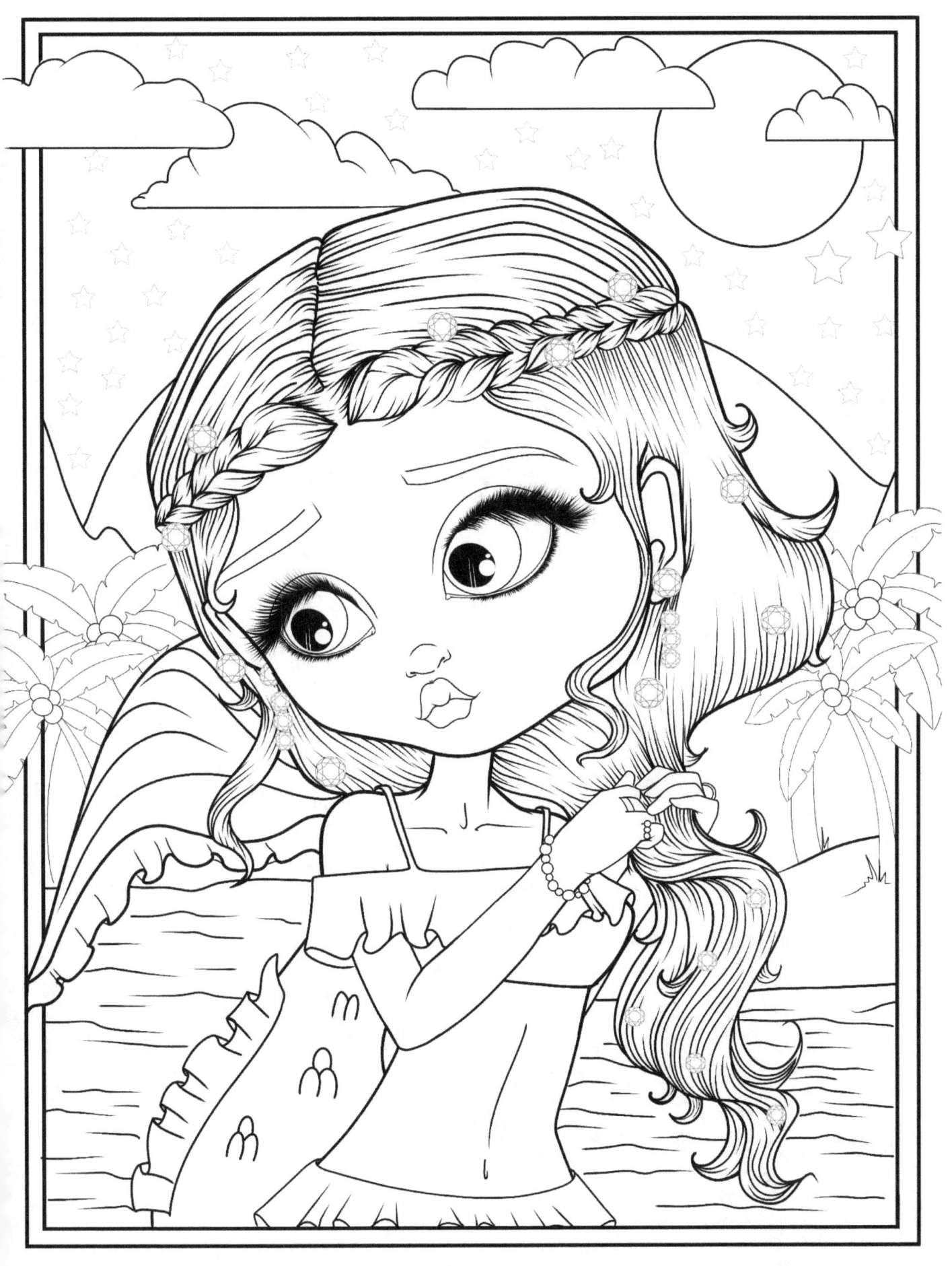

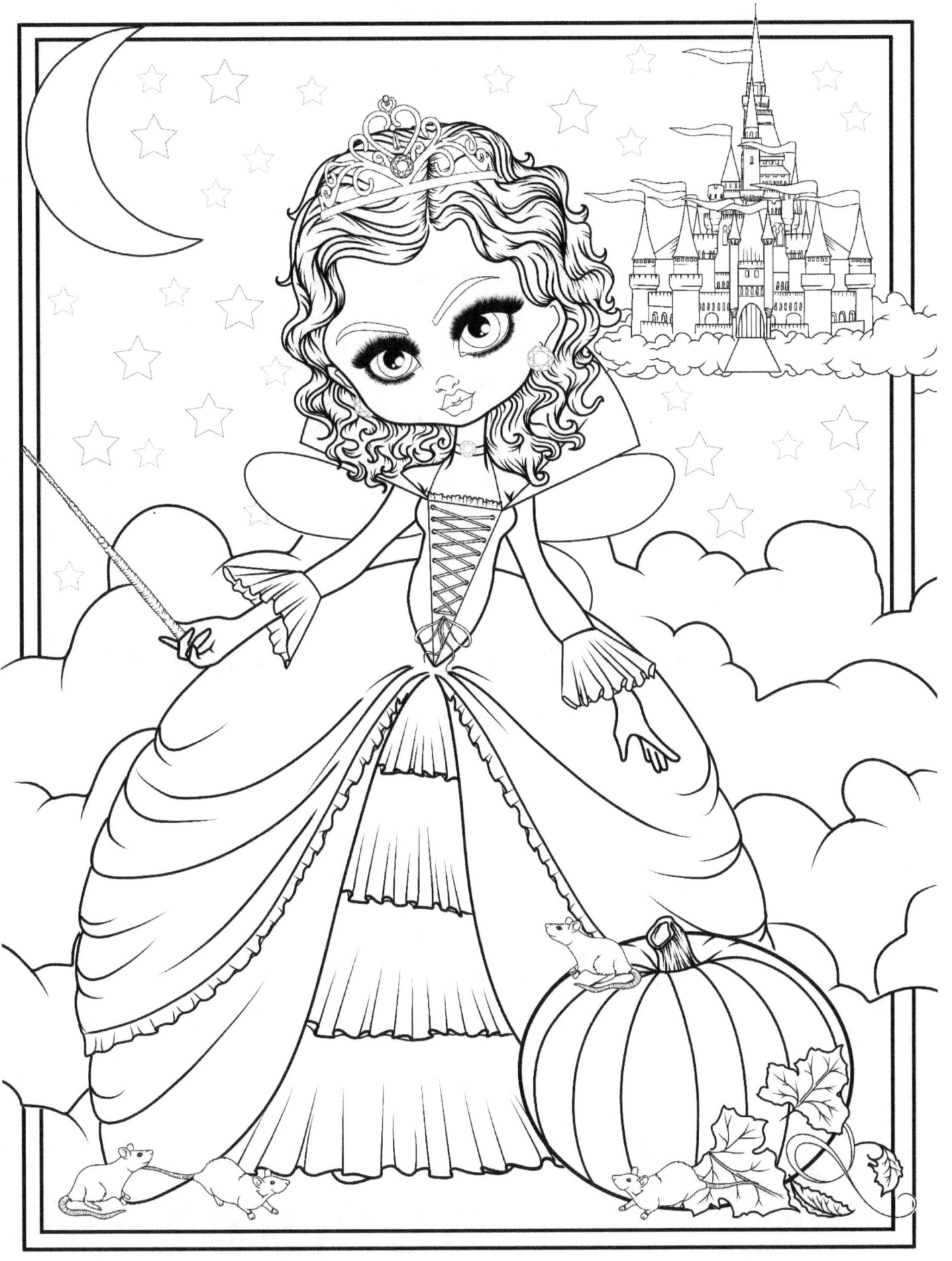

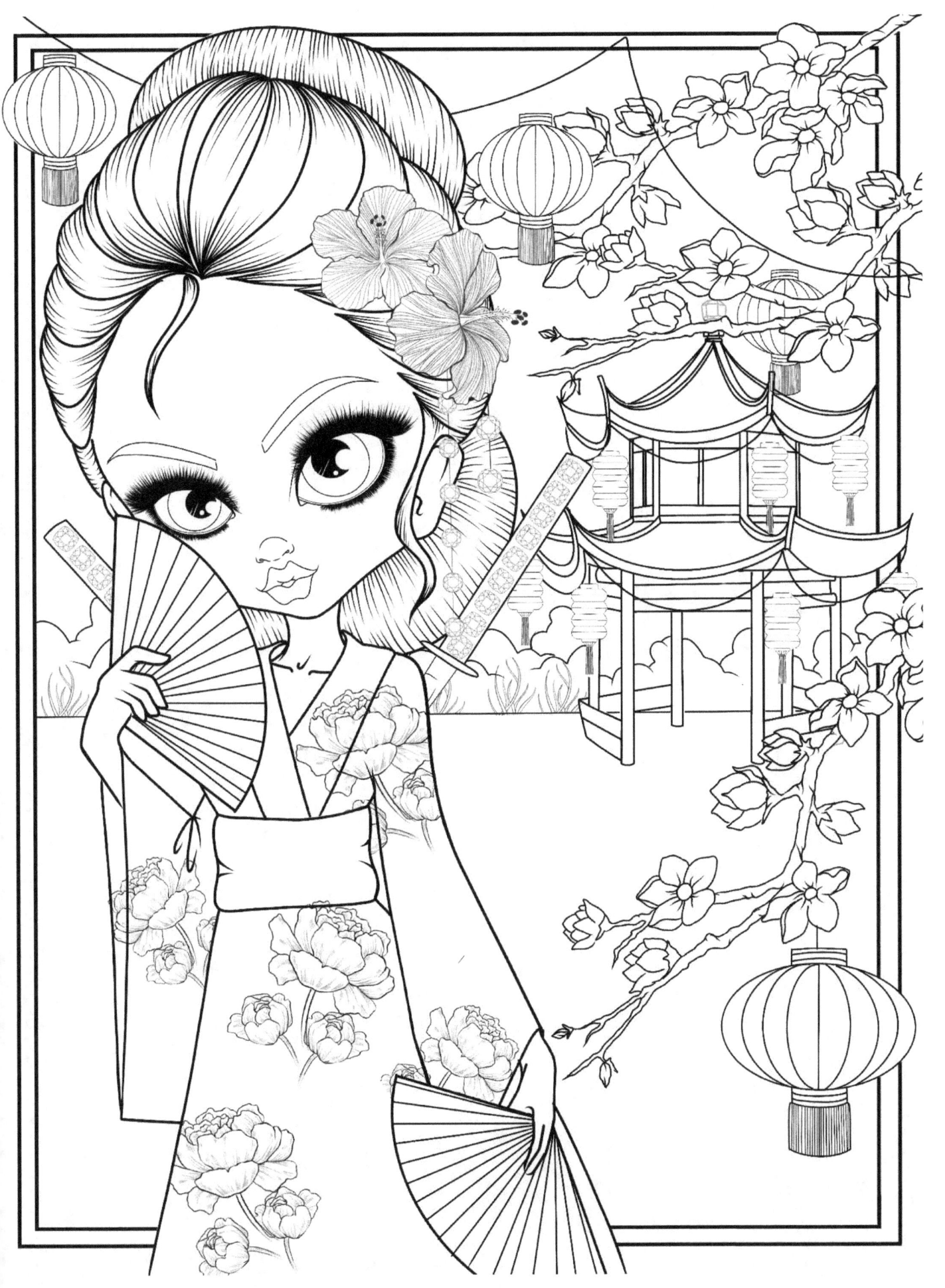

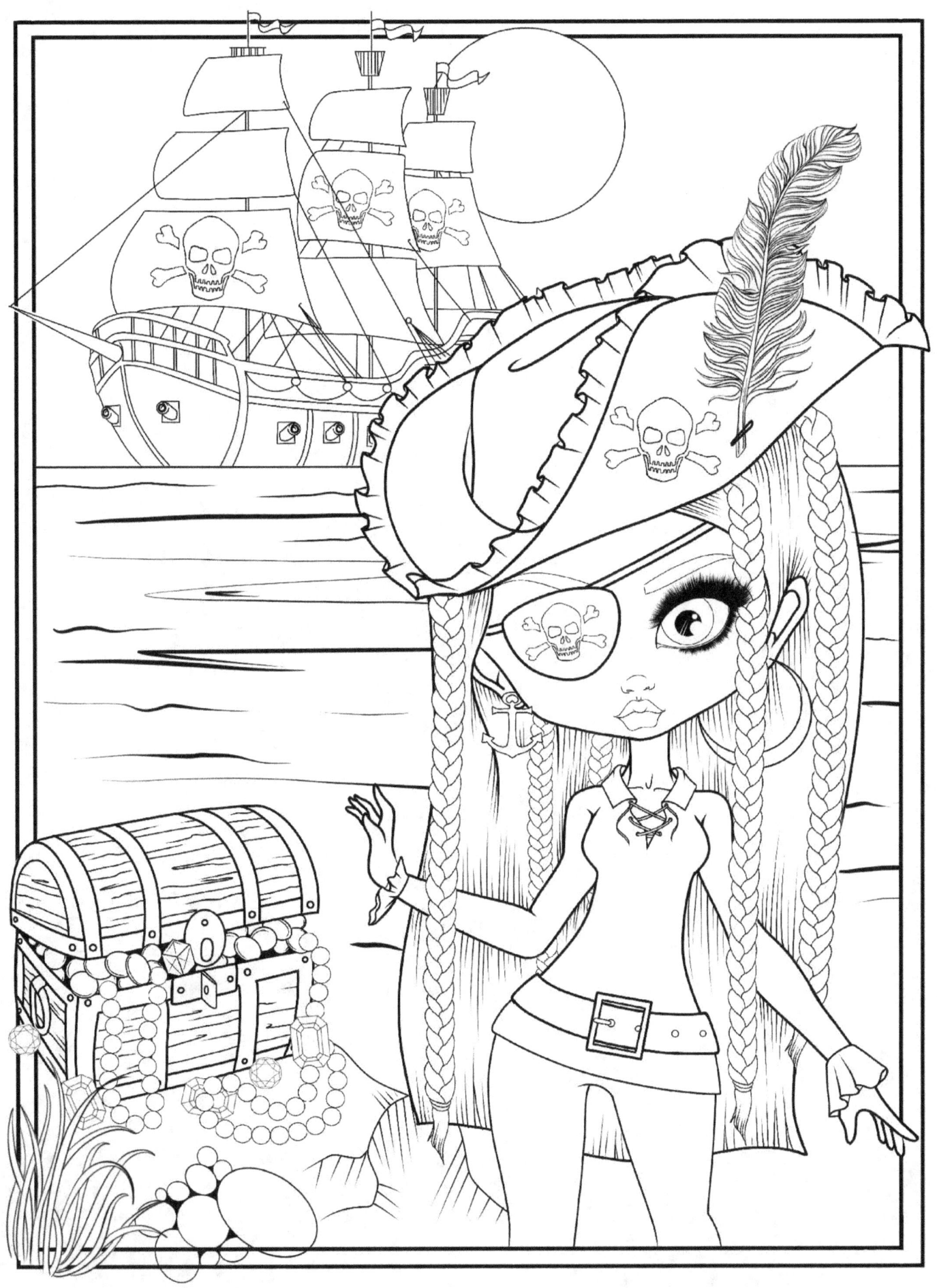

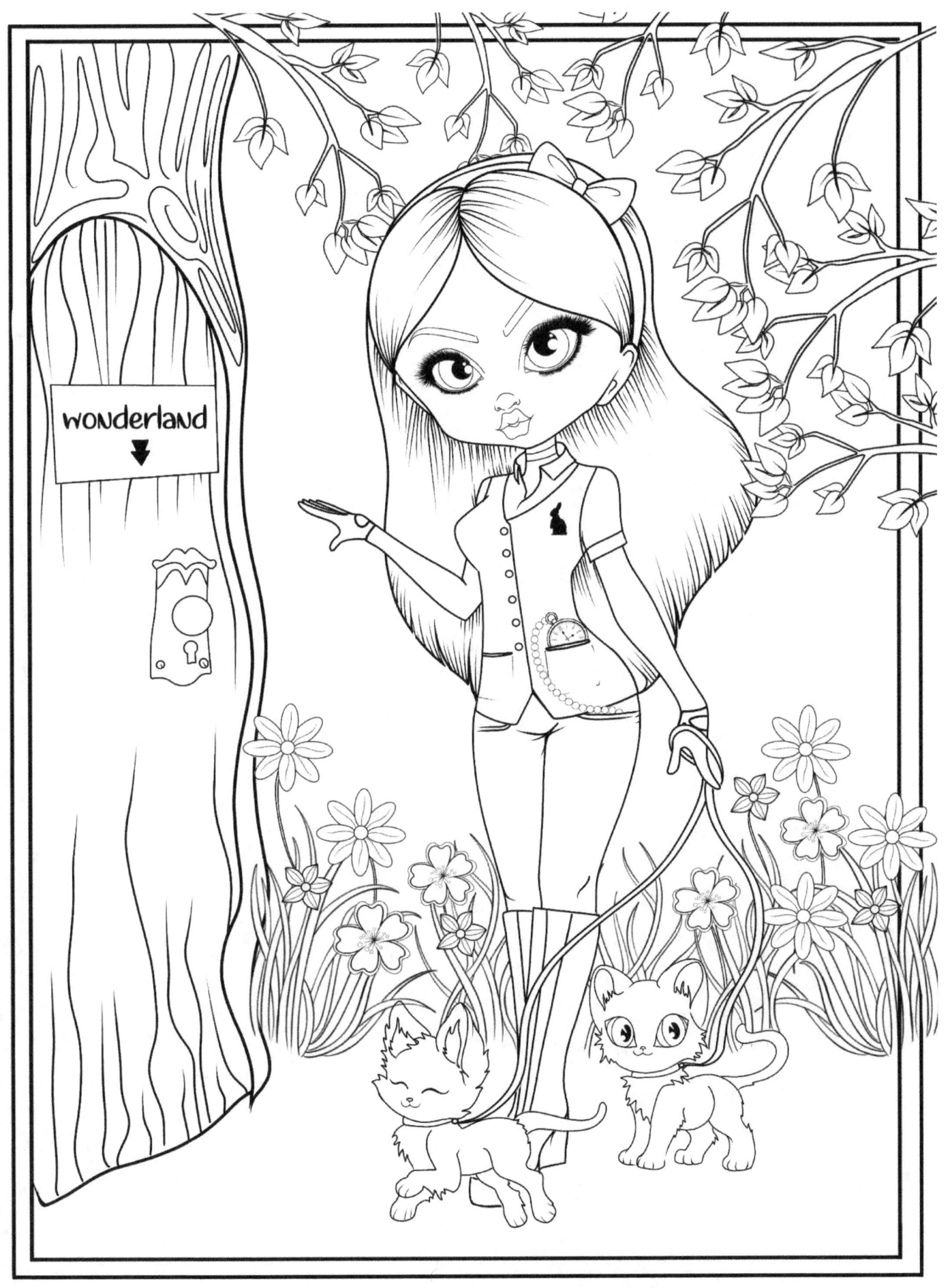

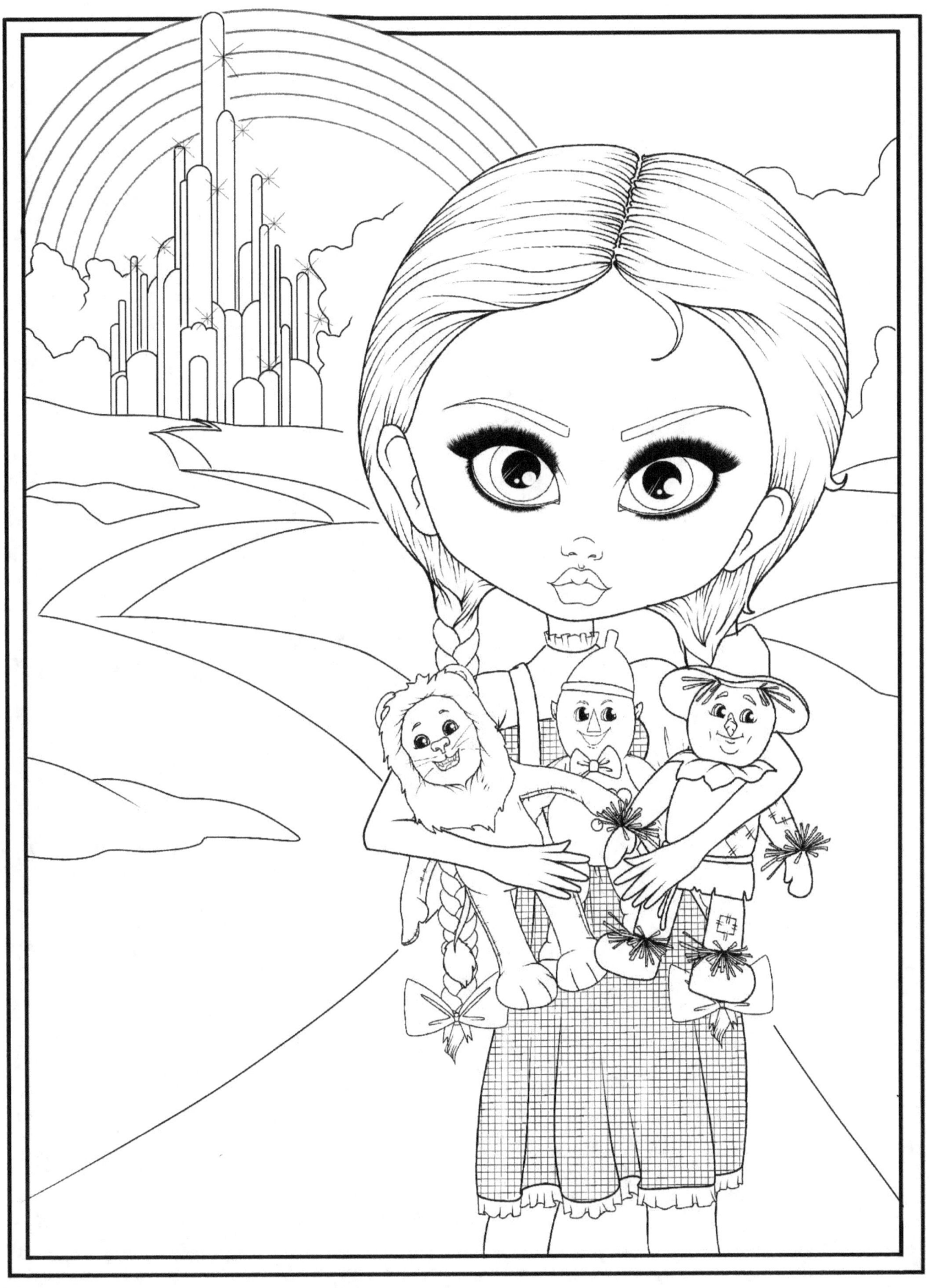

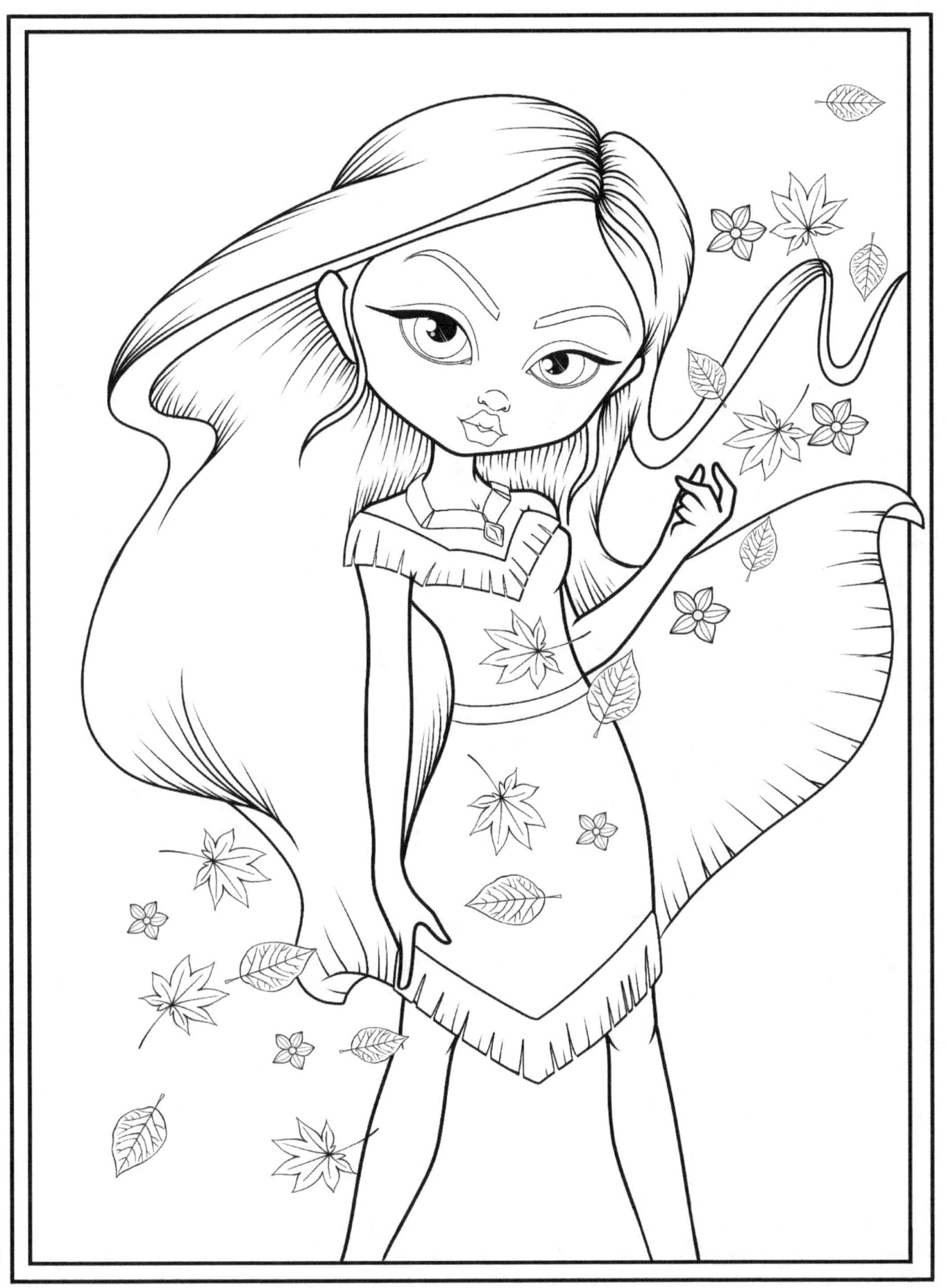

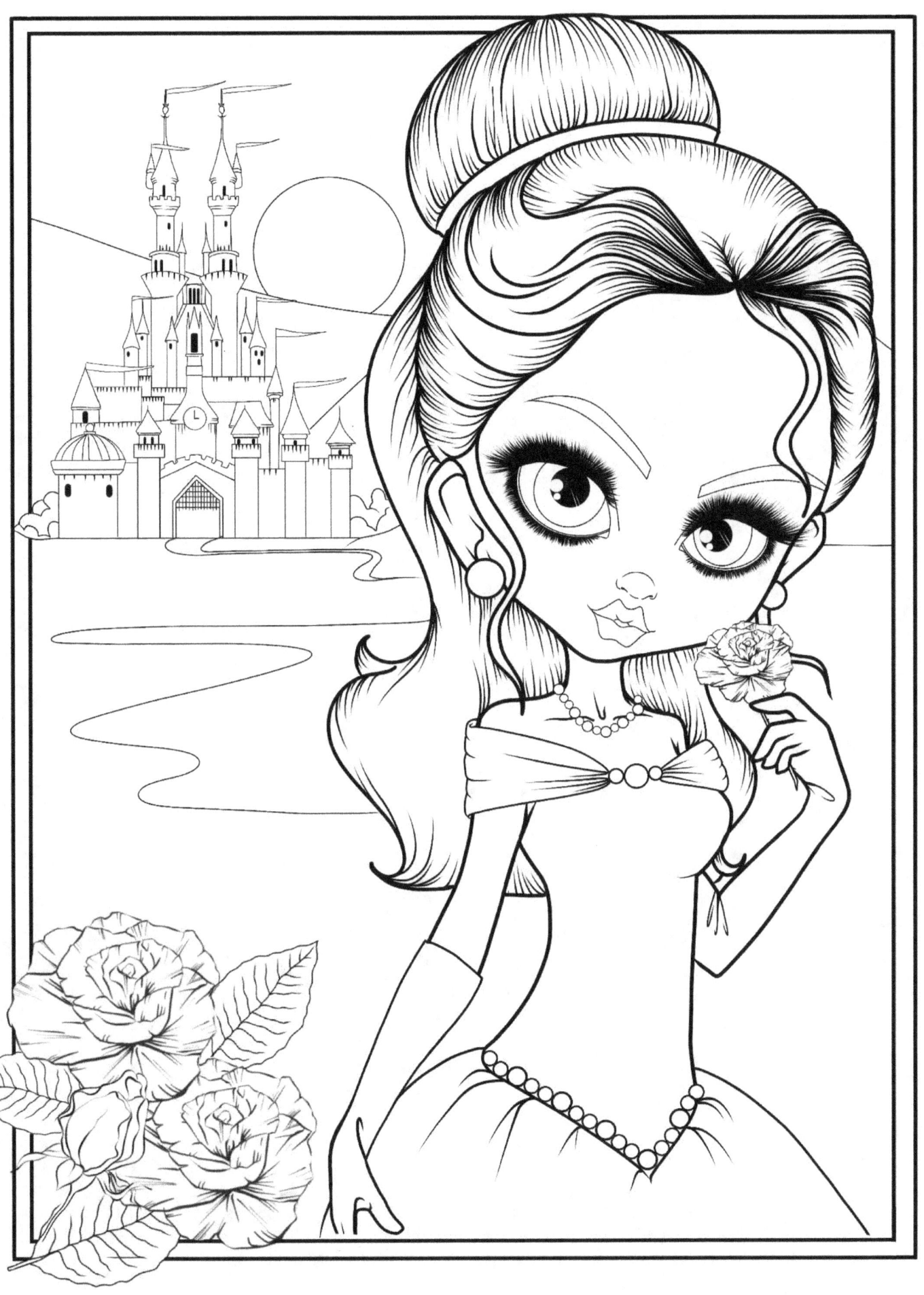

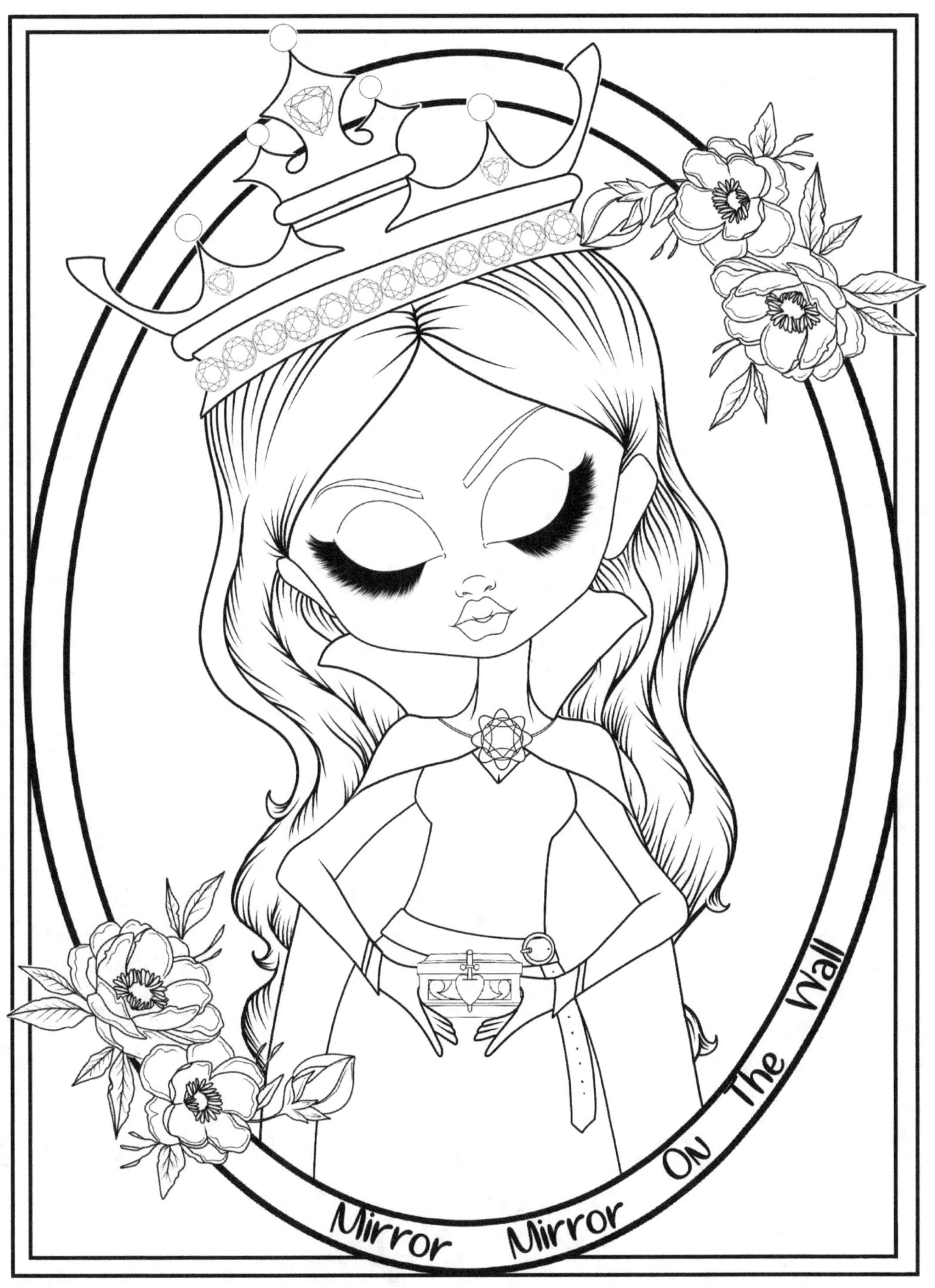

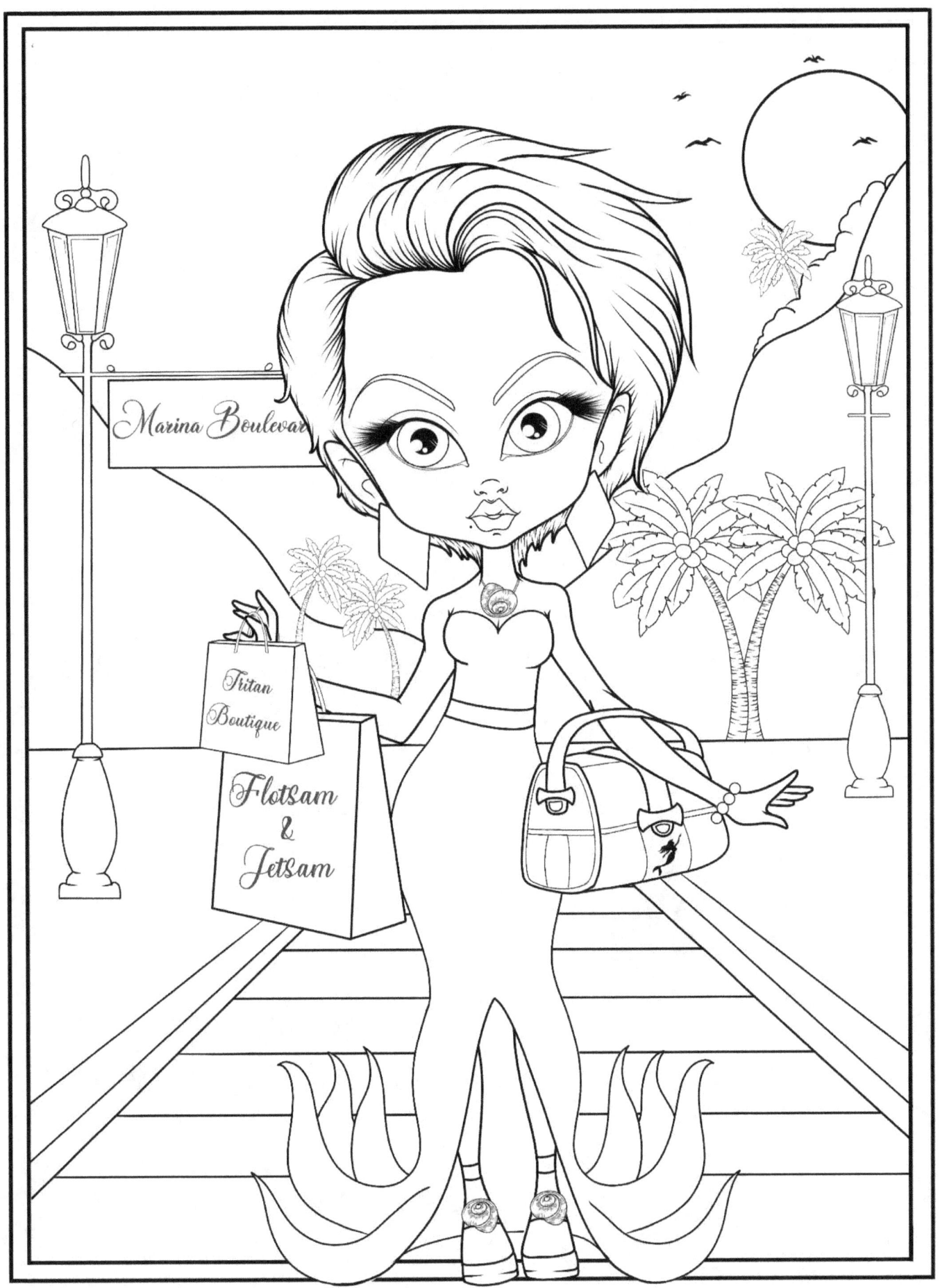

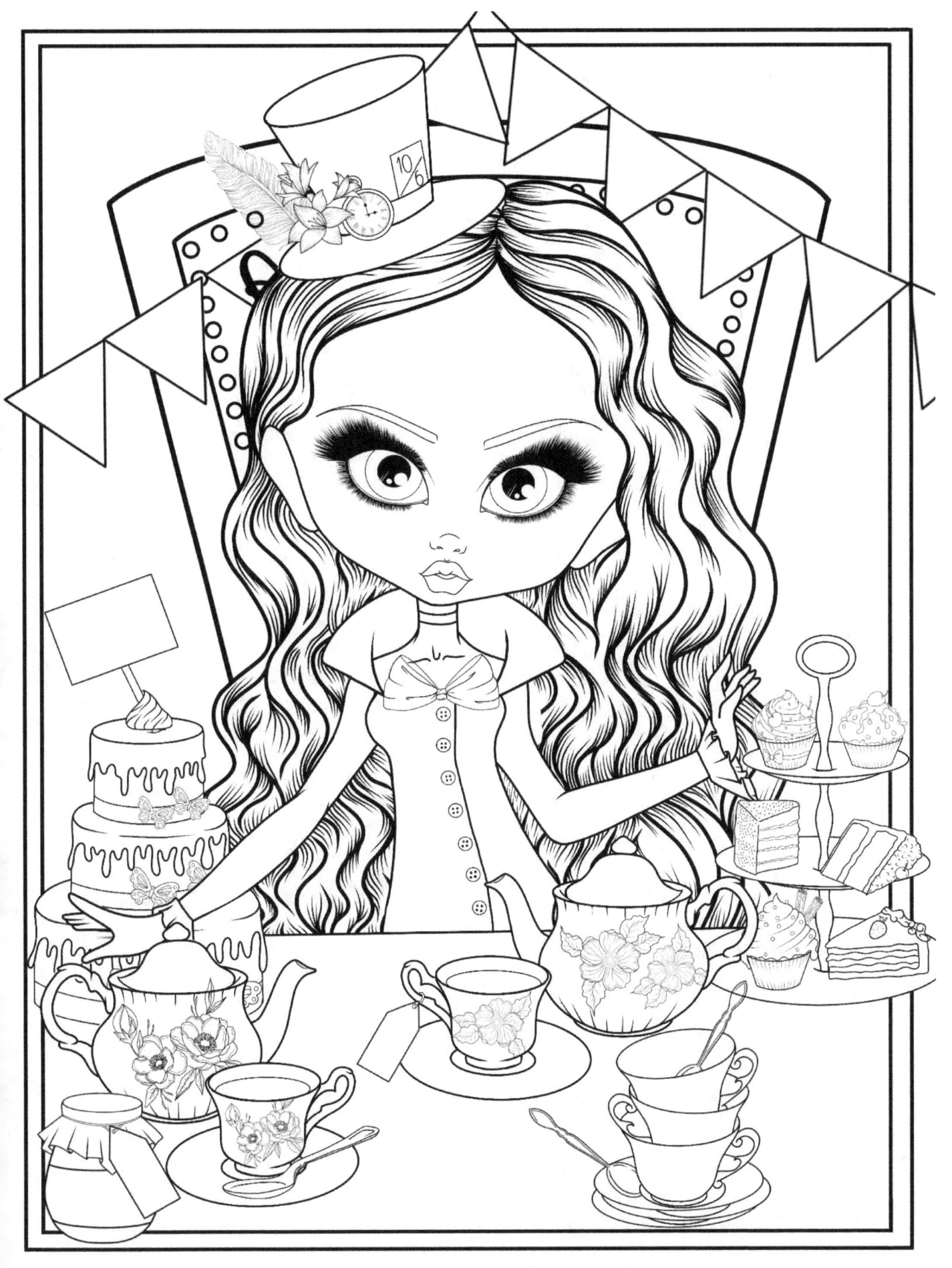

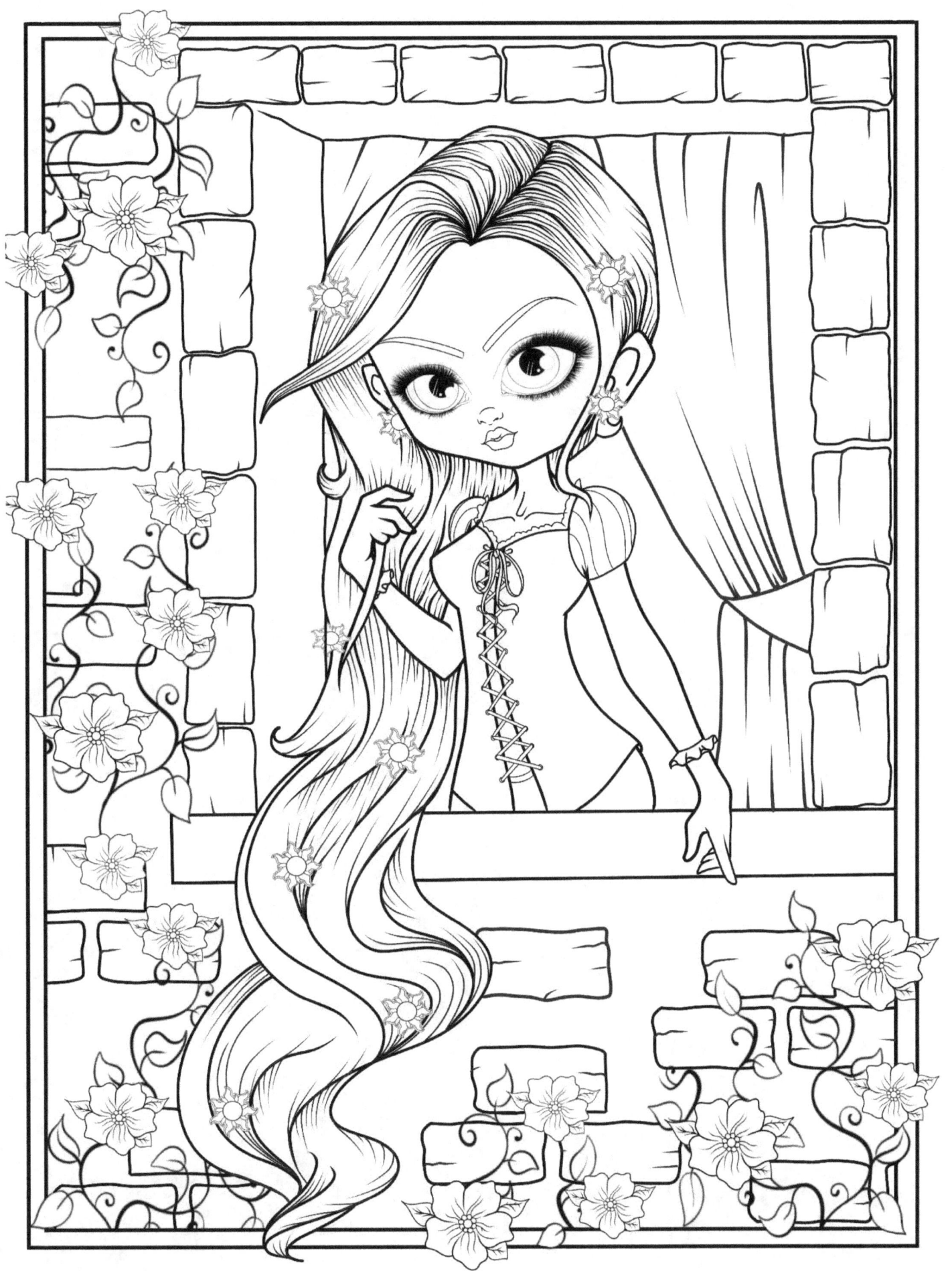

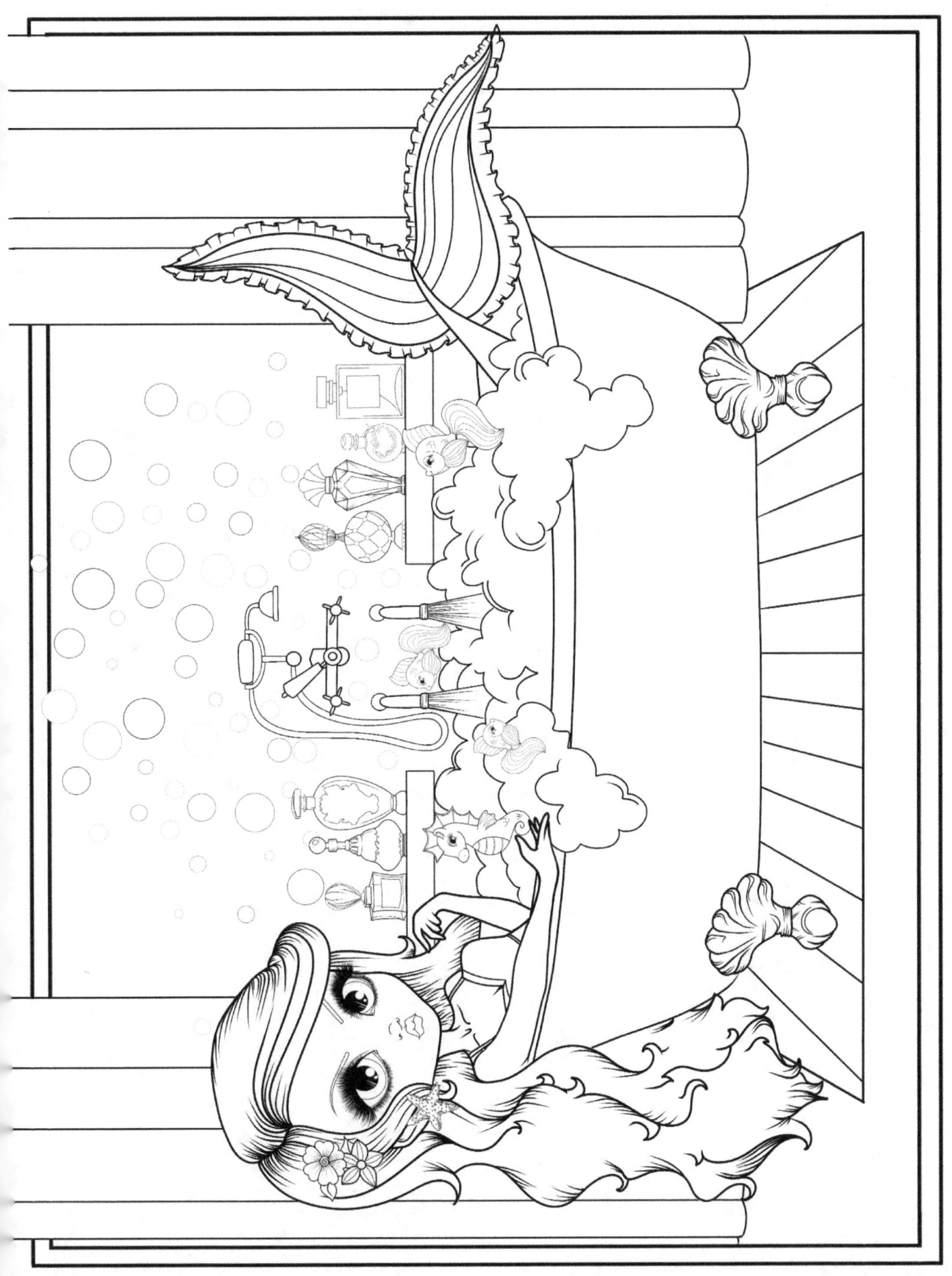

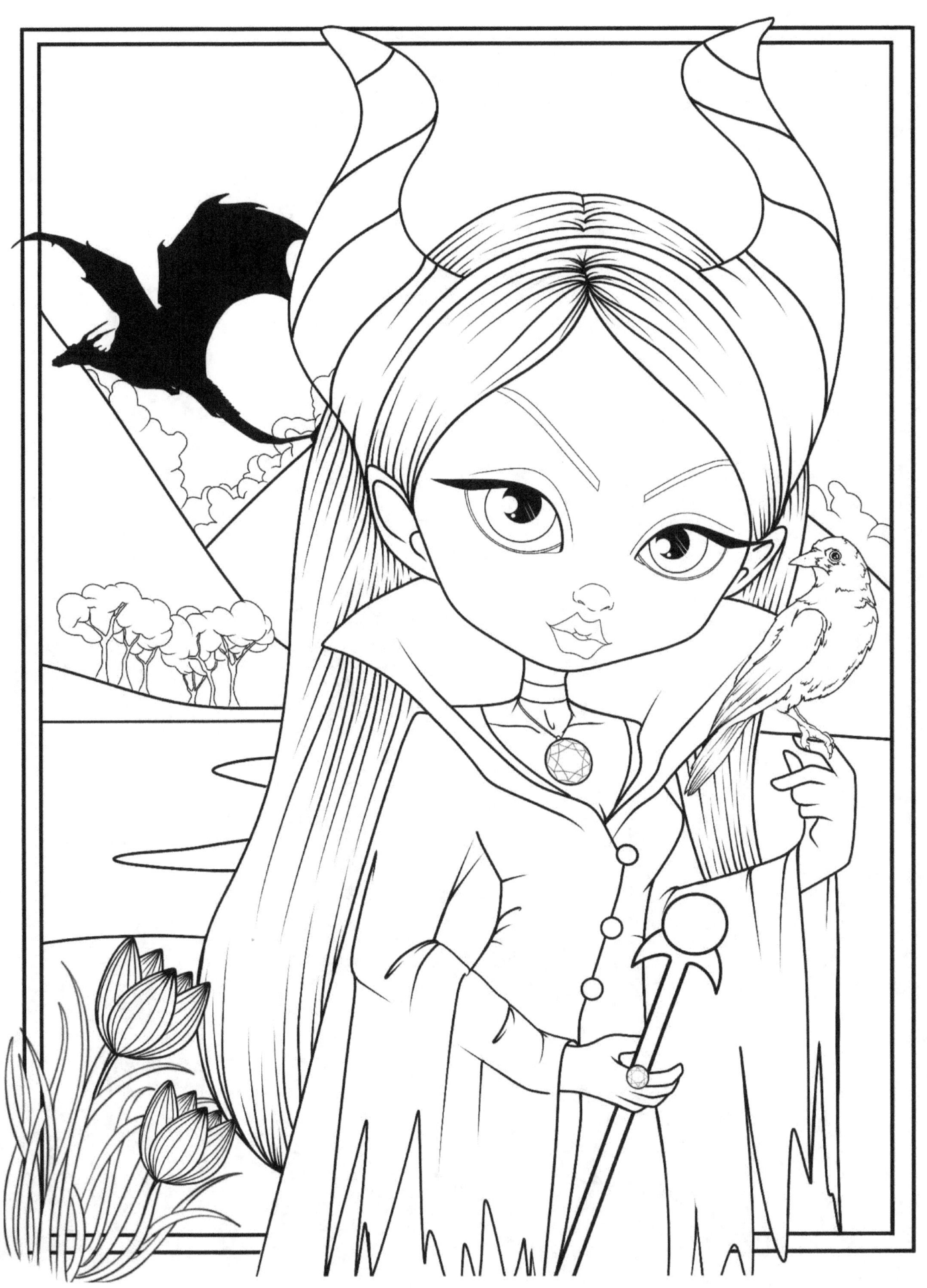

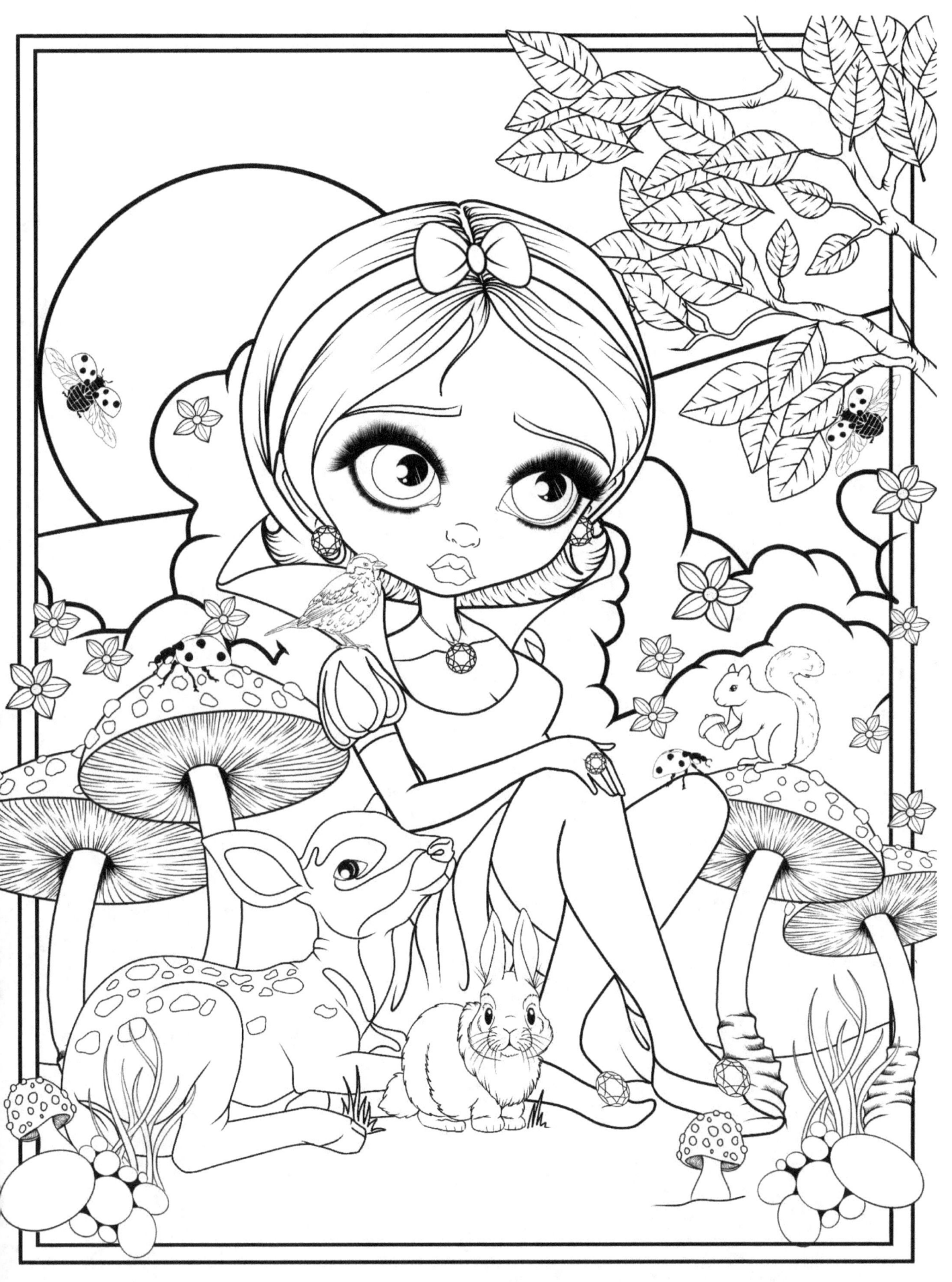

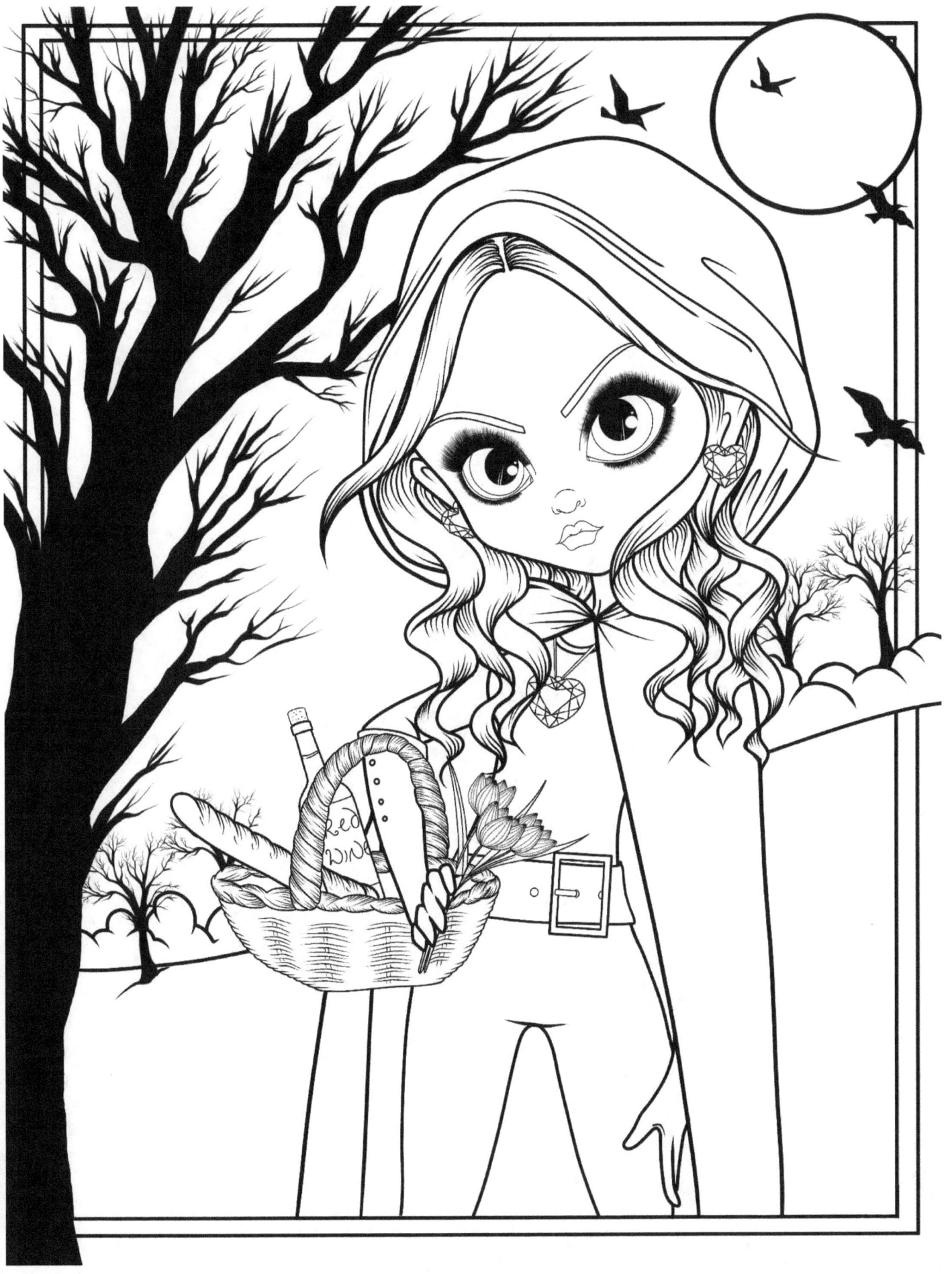

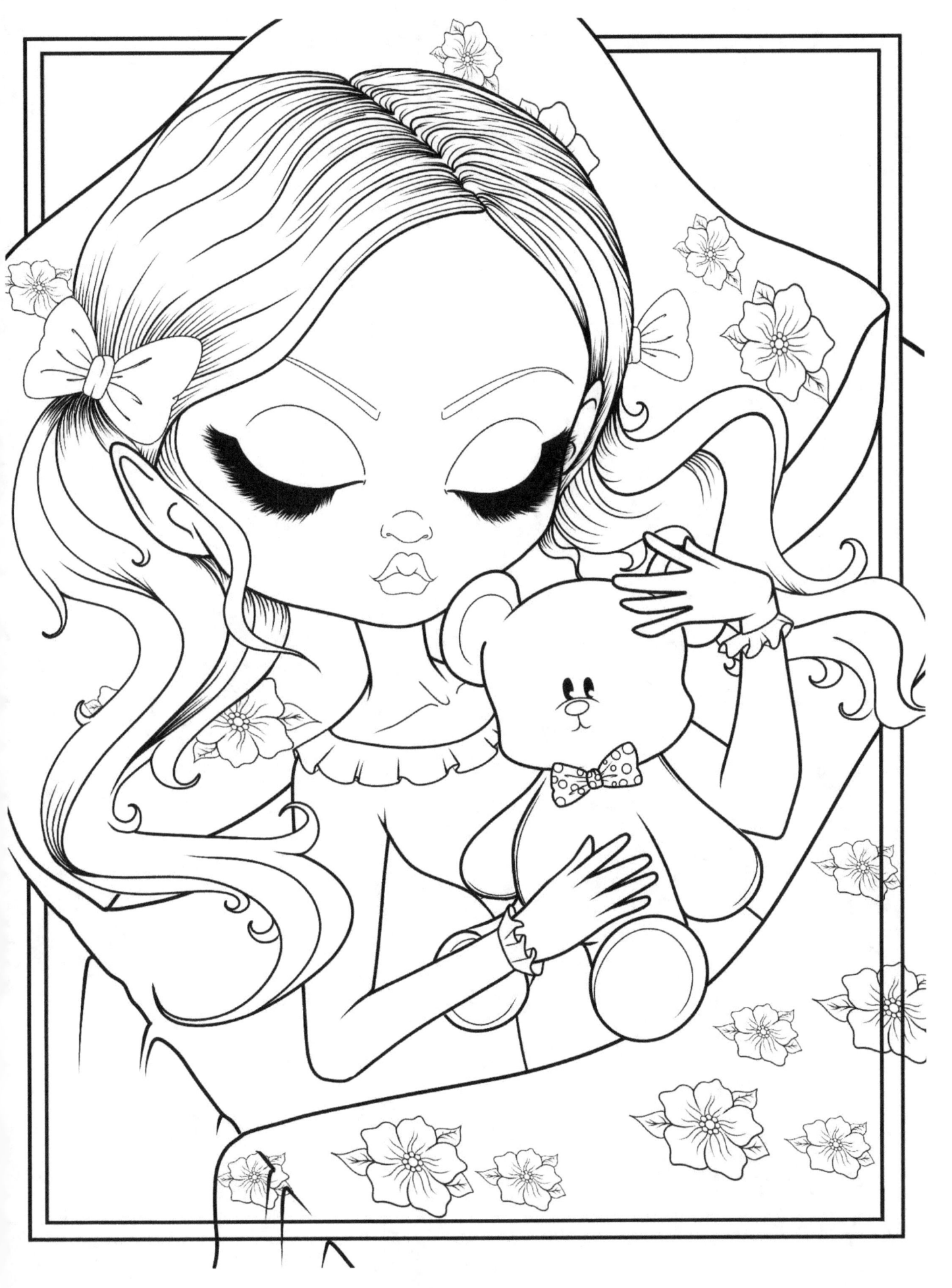

StoryBook Darlings

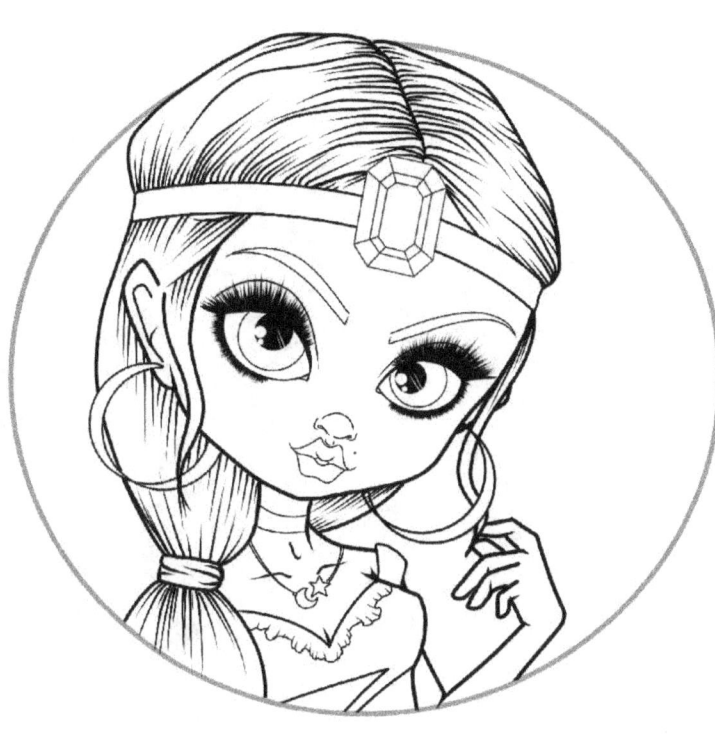

Zara

Maria

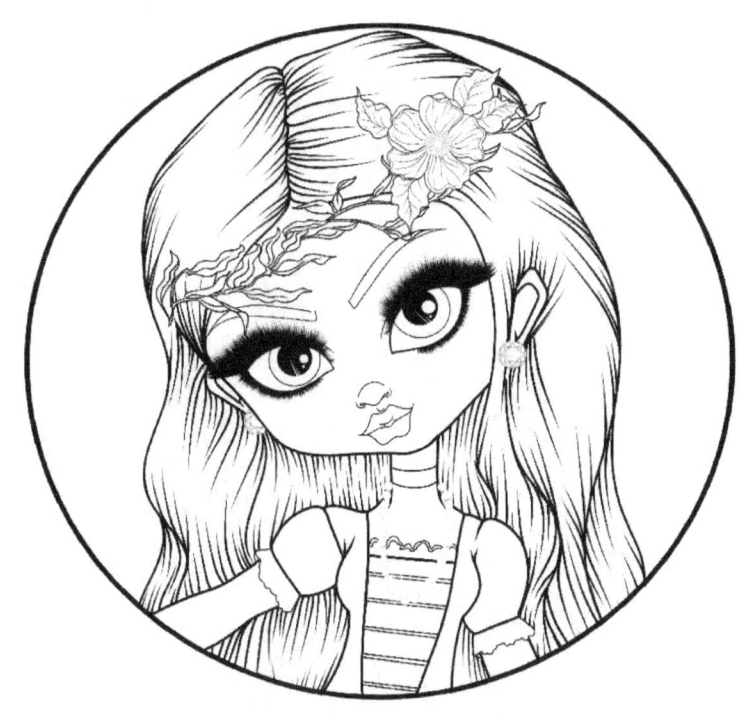

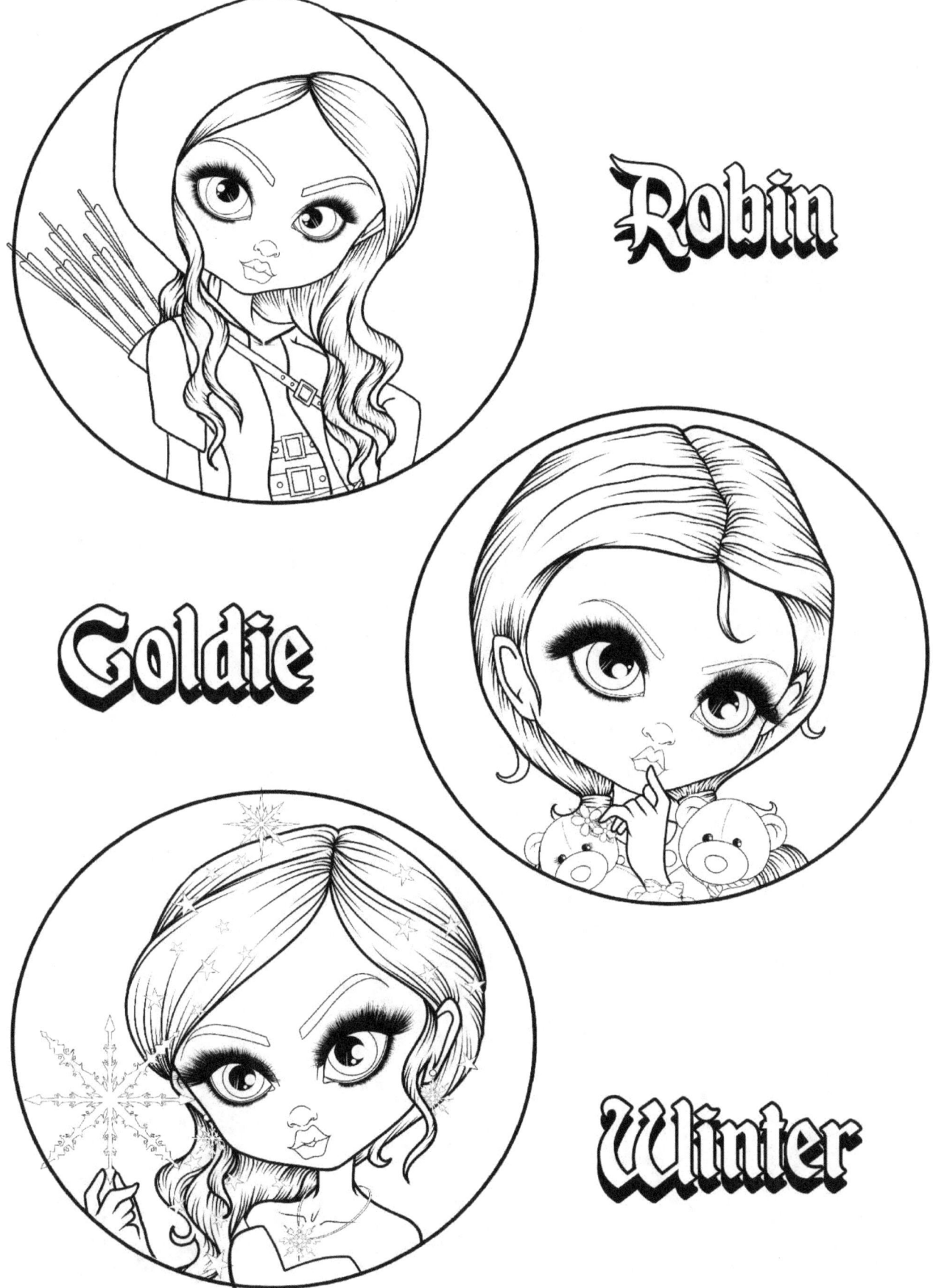

Robin

Goldie

Winter

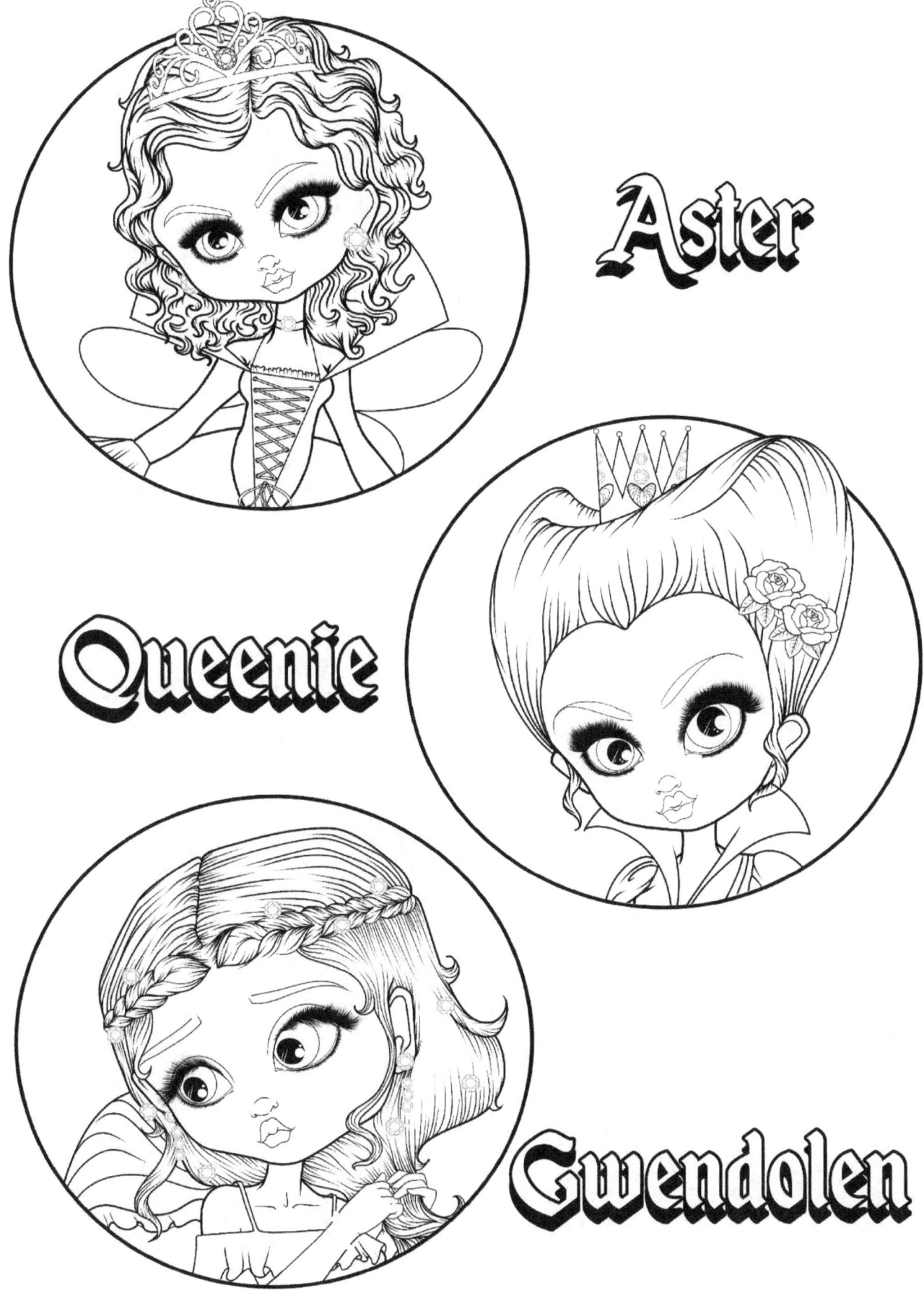

Aster

Queenie

Gwendolen

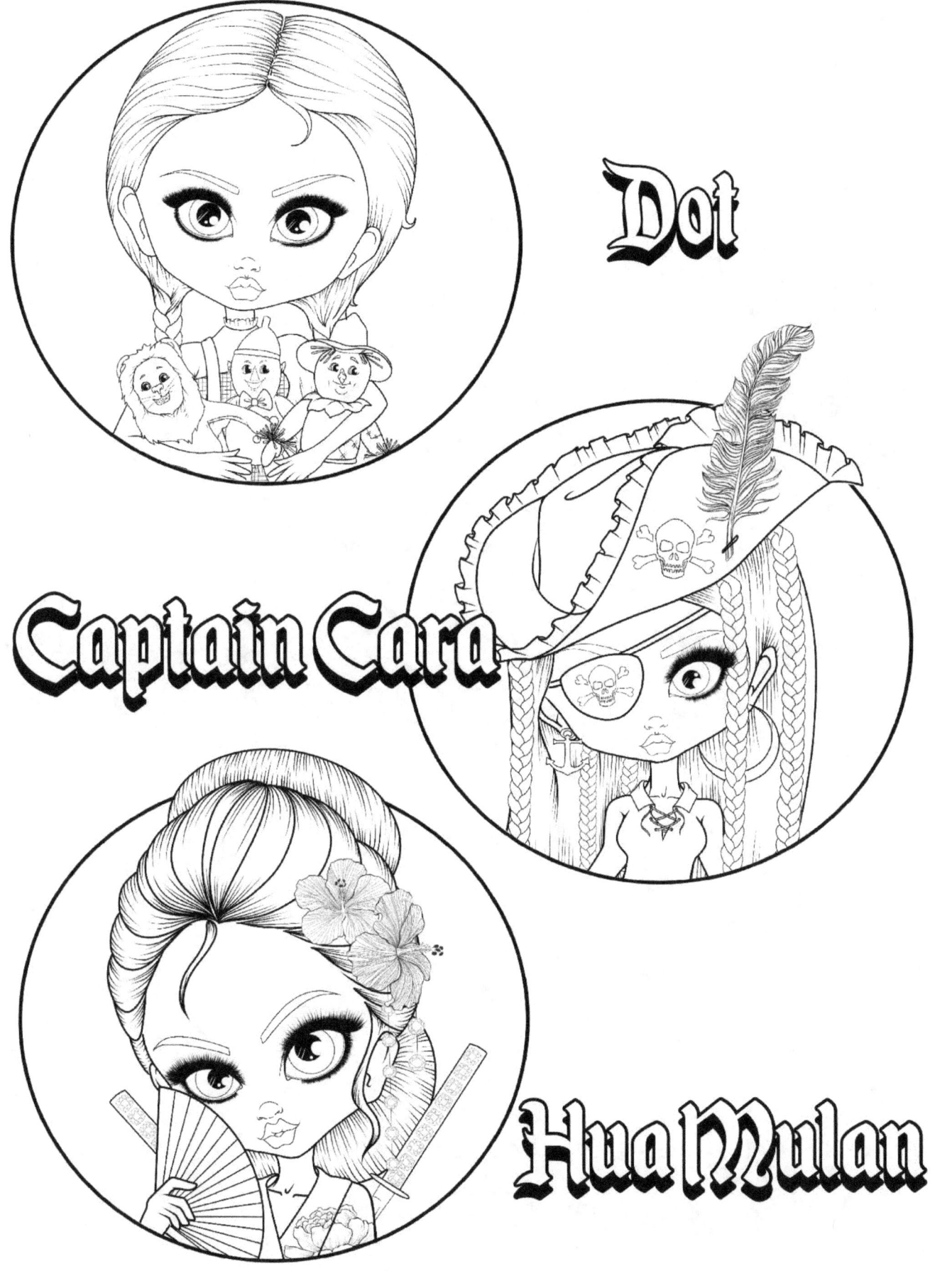

Dot

Captain Cara

HuaMulan

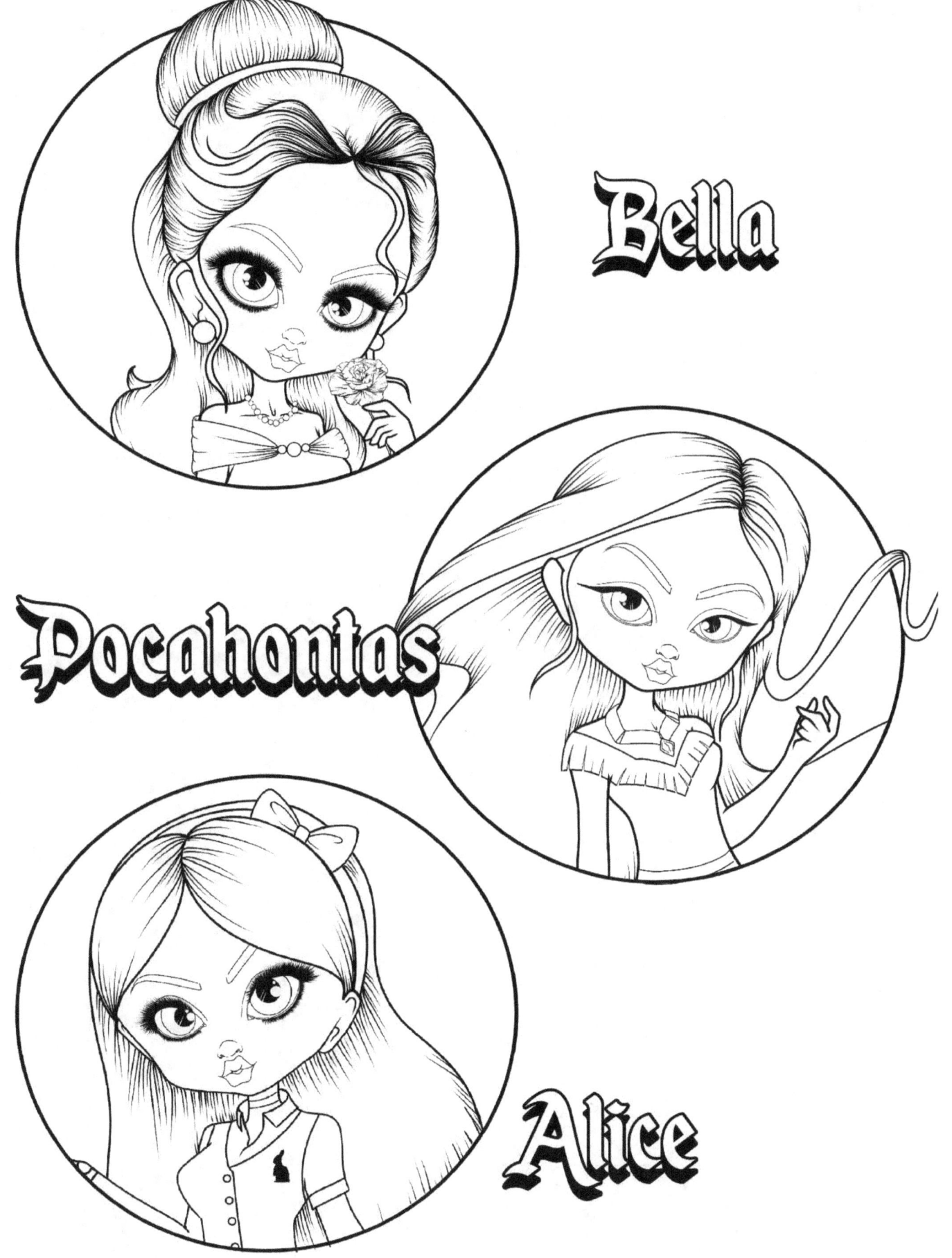

Bella

Pocahontas

Alice

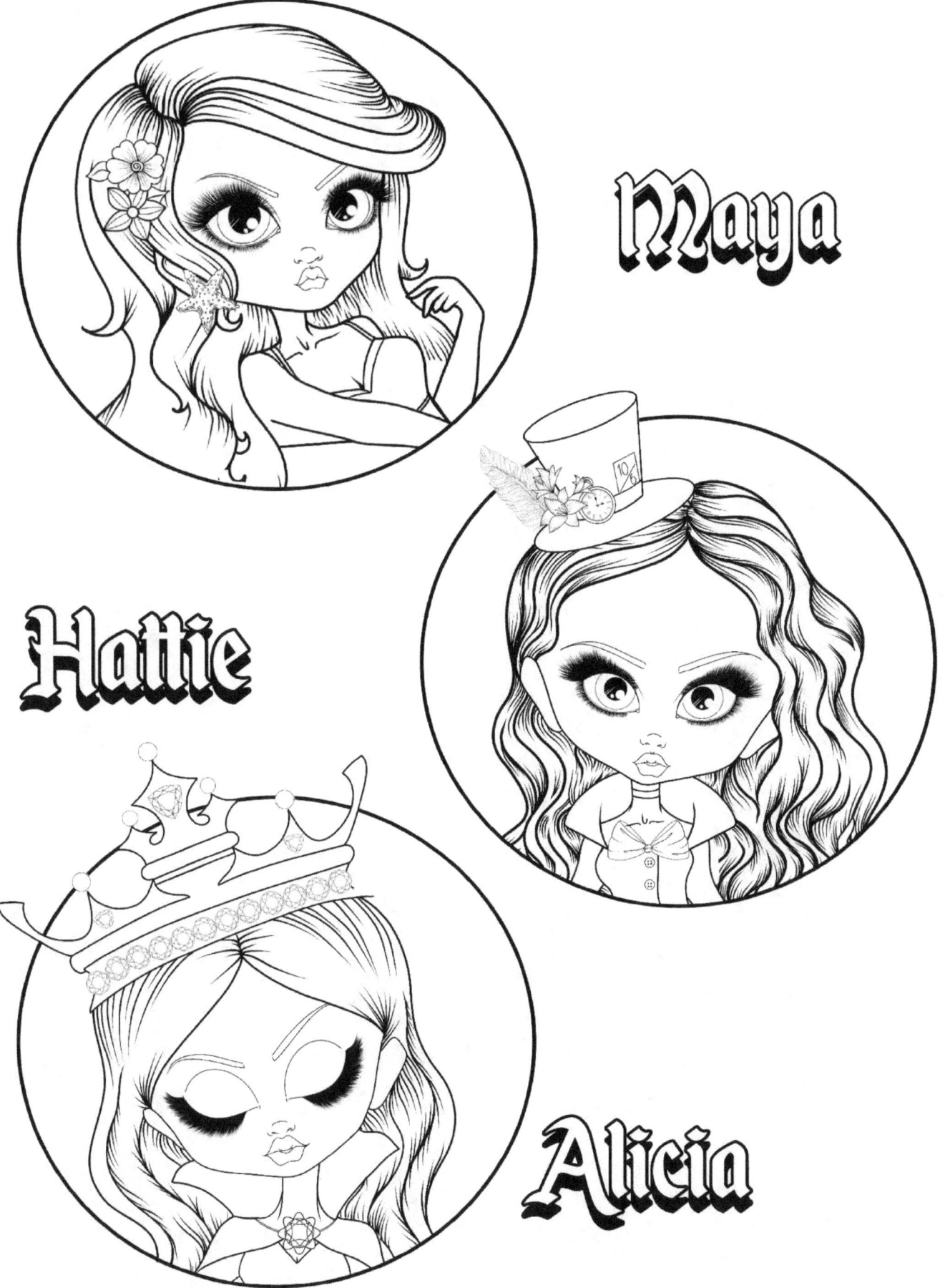

Maya

Hattie

Alicia

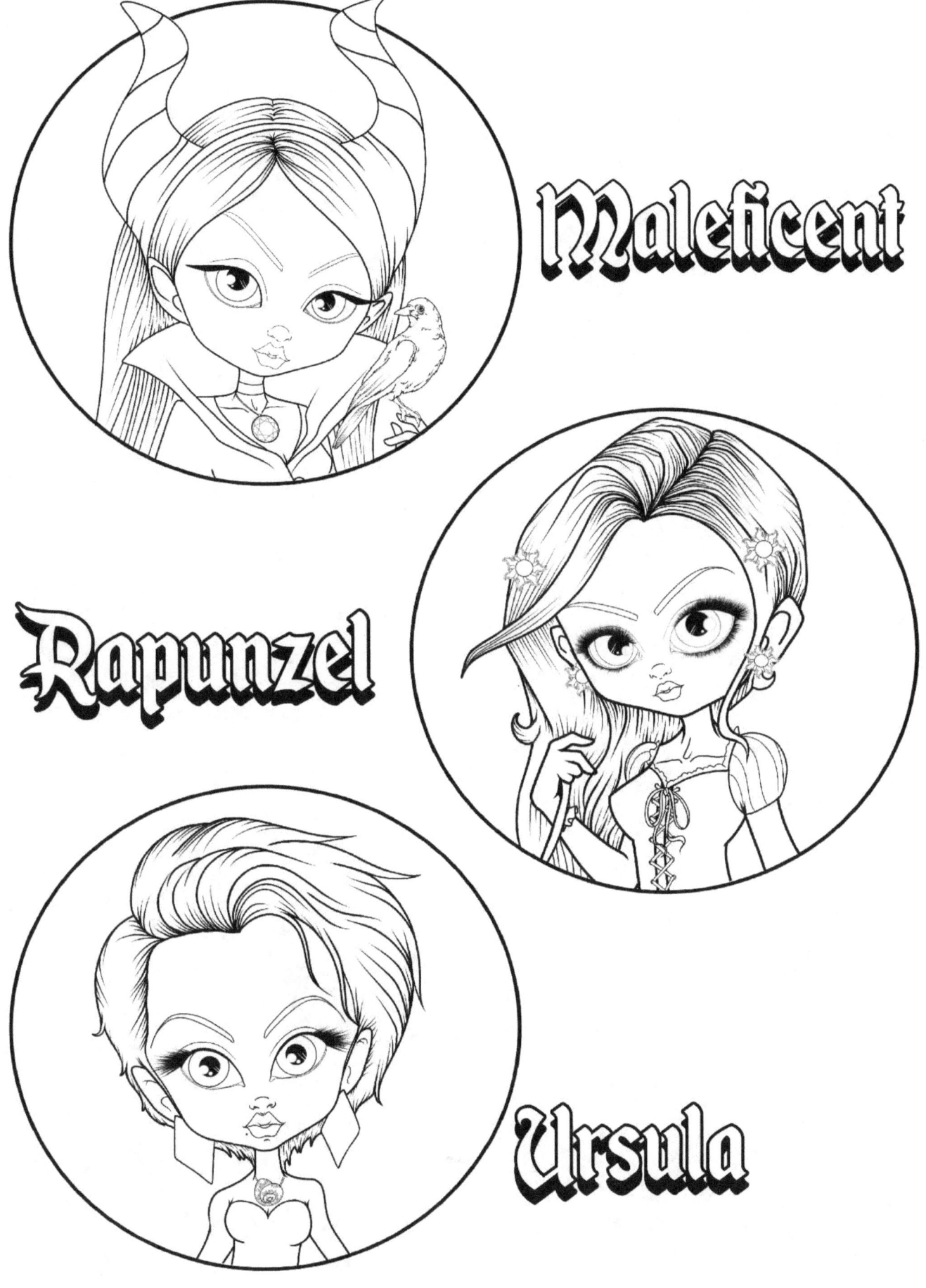

Maleficent

Rapunzel

Ursula

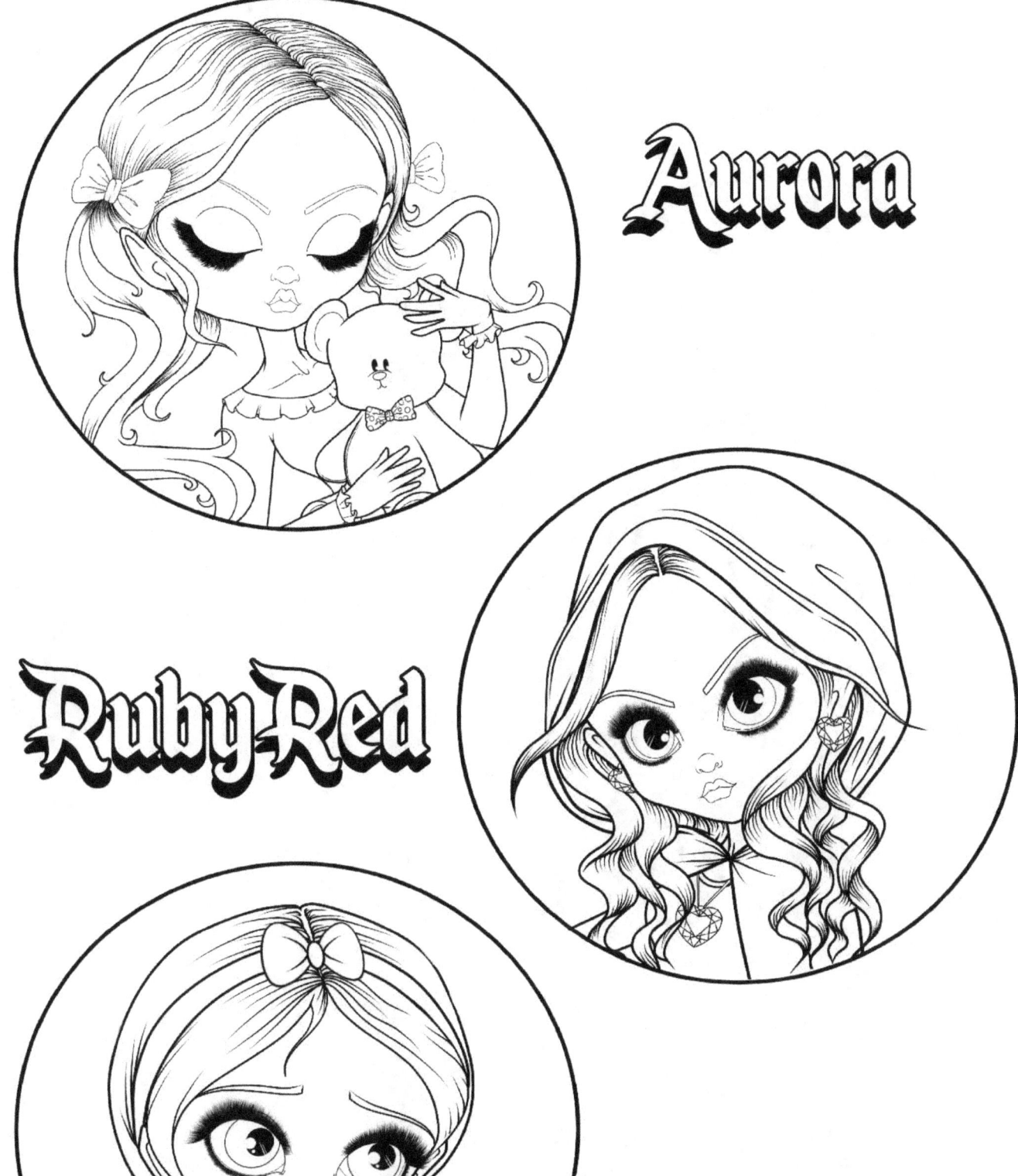

Aurora

Ruby Red

Snow

Skin tone practise

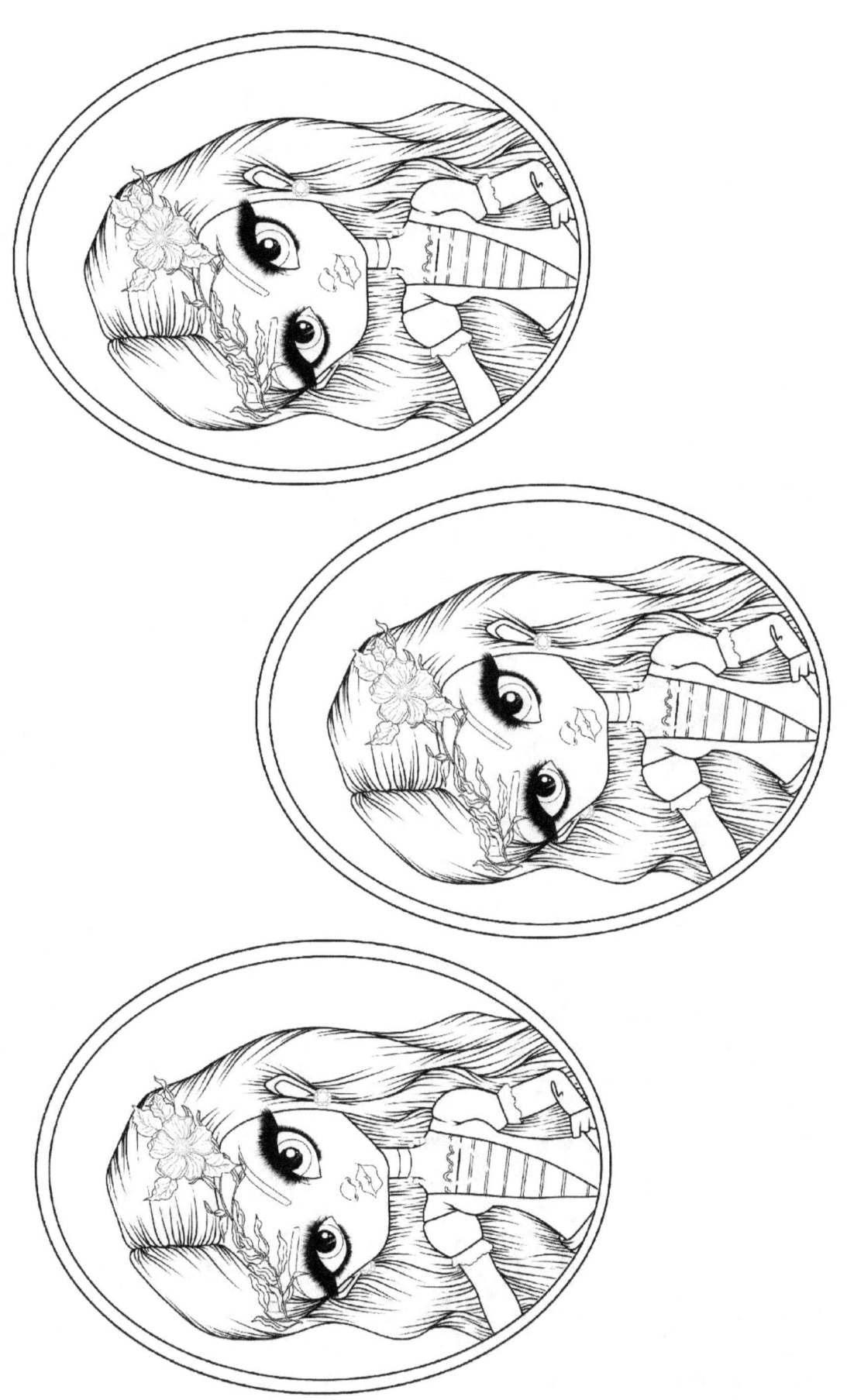

Skin tone practise

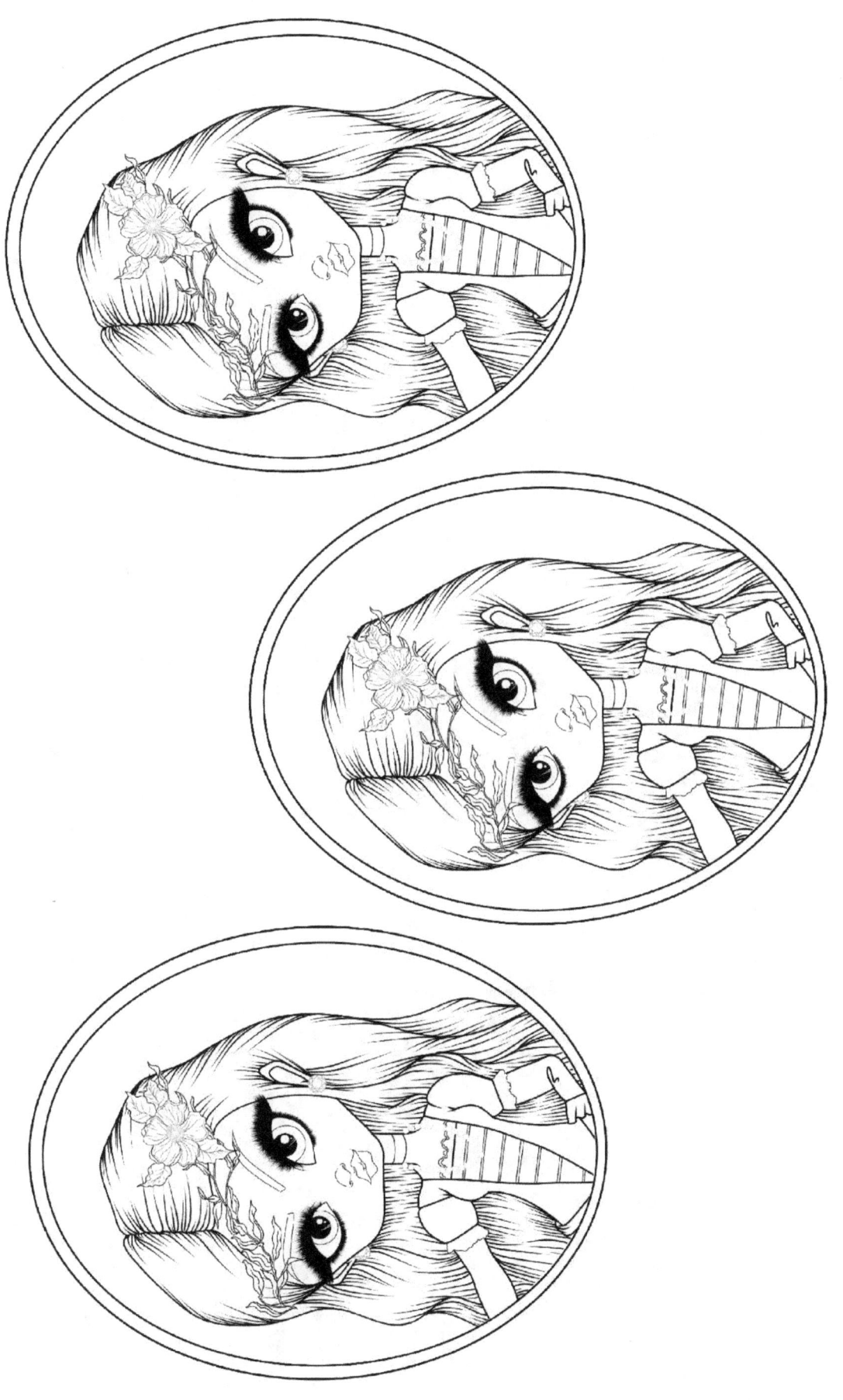

Colour swatch index

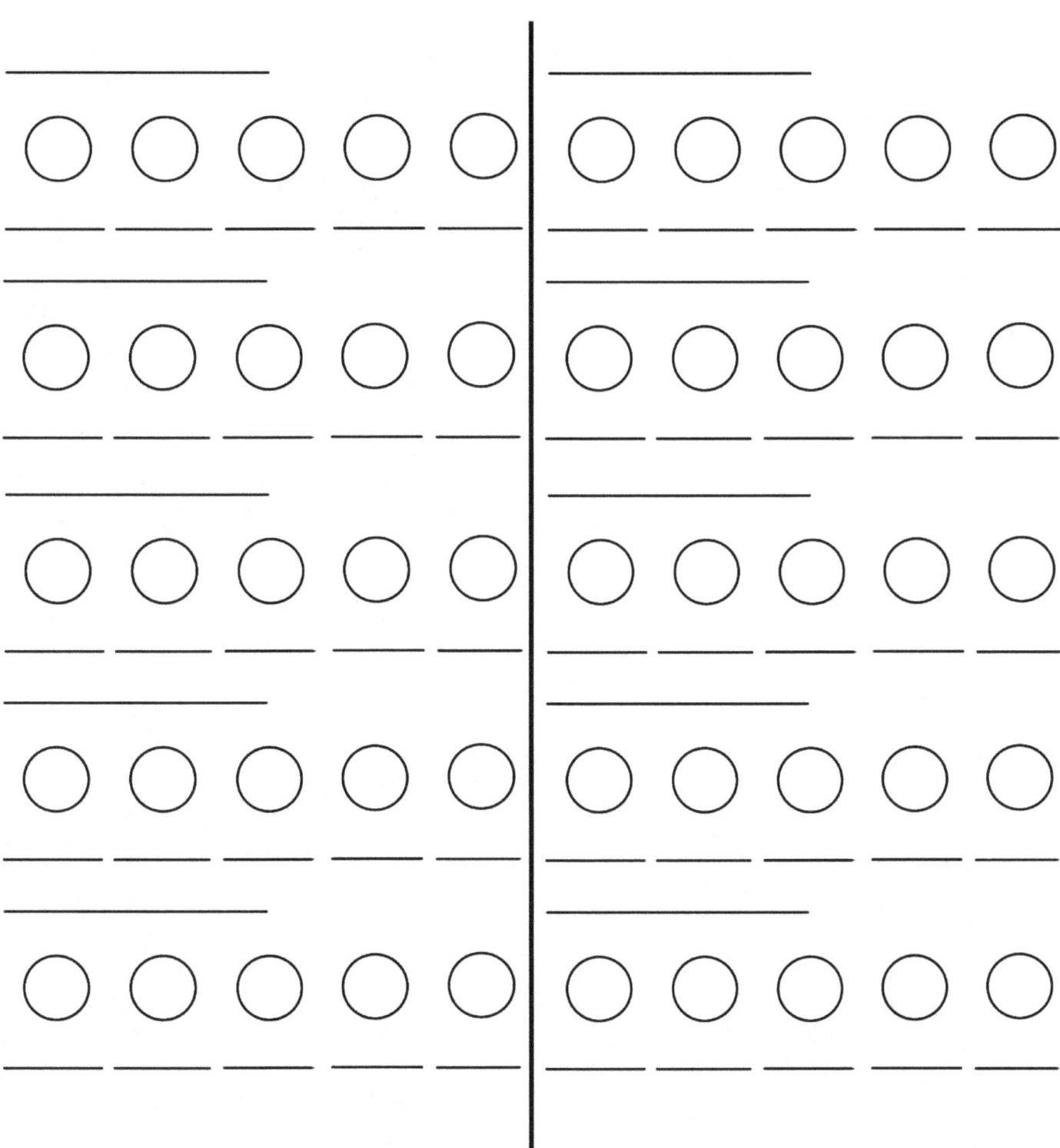

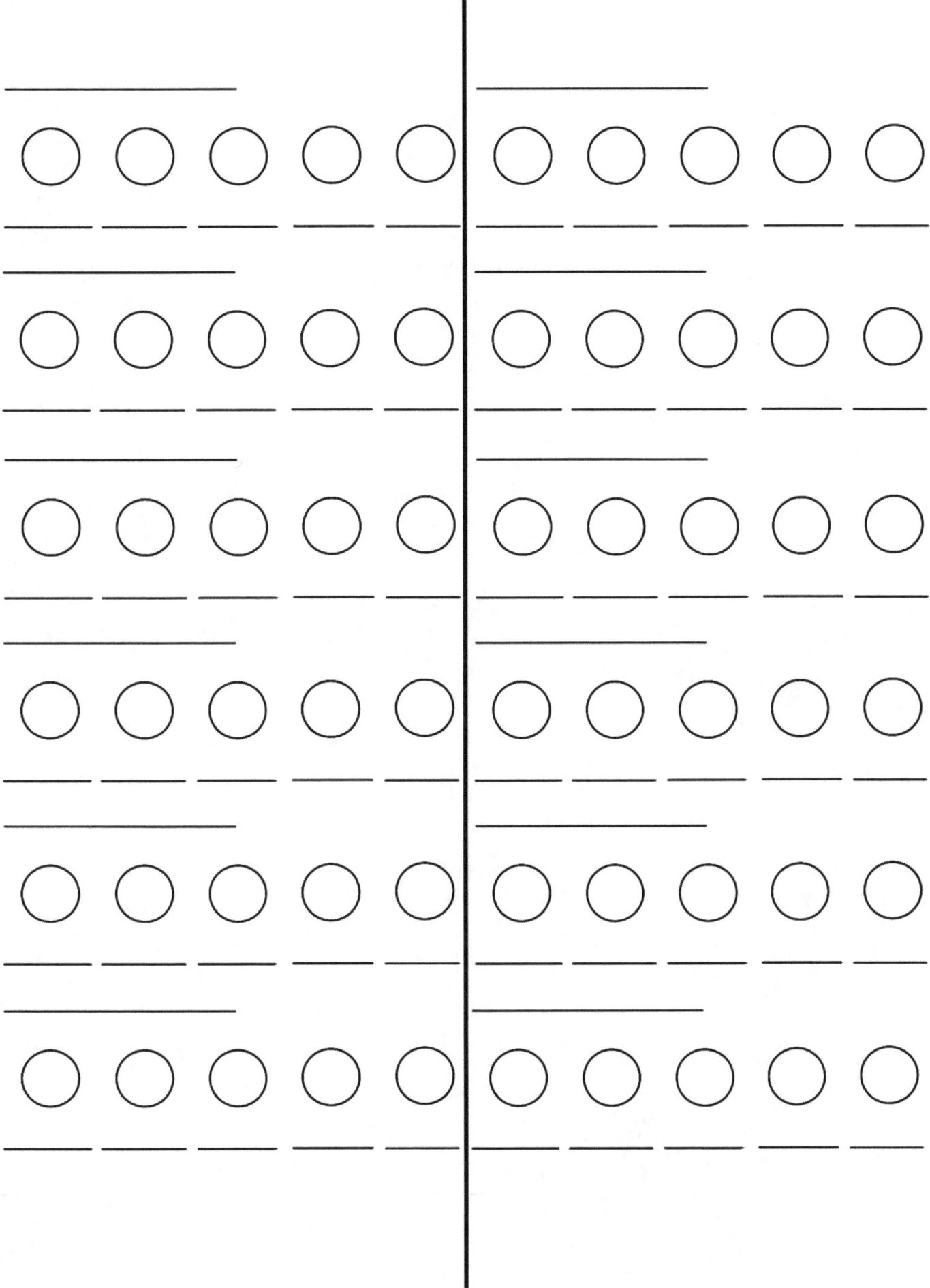

www.ingramcontent.com/pod-product-compliance
Lightning Source LLC
Chambersburg PA
CBHW080820170526
45158CB00009B/2480